For You

Andreas Seidl

Handover of Power

Global Version

Volume 19: Foreign Affairs

Imprint

Bibliographic information of the German National Library:
The German National Library lists this publication in the
German National Bibliography; detailed bibliographic data
are available on the Internet at http://dnb.dnb.de.

© 2022 Dipl. Pol. Theodor Andreas Seidl

Cover: Christiane Ebrecht
Translation: DeepL, Cologne
Production and publishing: BoD – Books on Demand,
Norderstedt

ISBN: 978-3-7568-0044-5

Acknowledgements

My thanks go to my family and friends who have made me who I am today. Special thanks to all those who supported me in writing this book. I would like to thank all my classmates, teachers, fellow students, lecturers, demonstrators, activists, colleagues, companies and countries with whom I have had the privilege of sharing the experiences from which all the ideas in this book have emerged. I would like to thank the staff of Books on Demand for their kind helpfulness. I thank the citizens of Seligenstadt for the harmony and solidarity in which I was able to write.

Foreword

This policy concept contains a variety of proposals for possible political reforms. It can be peacefully and democratically adapted to any current political system of any state in the world, but also to political systems in families, clubs, associations or companies. Wherever humans make or submit to rules that manage living together, the following proposals can be helpful. Readers who find the proposals so helpful that they would like to implement them together with like-minded people can contact the author. The contact form on the last page can be used for this purpose.

Faults and defects

I ask for your understanding that this volume was not professionally proofread. I could only afford professional proofreading for the summary. Spelling errors and unfortunate phrasing may therefore occur. As soon as this volume has sold enough to pay for a professional proofreading, it will be done. After that, a new edition will be published.

English version

Please understand that this volume has been translated automatically. I could only afford a professional translation for the summary. Poor wording and spelling errors may therefore occur. In case of doubt, the German version shall prevail. As soon as this volume has sold enough to pay for a professional translation, it will be done. After that, a new edition will be published. It was more important to me that no one in the world should have an information advantage than individual translation errors in the complete work.

References
If something has been quoted directly, it is set in italics. If the headings contain footnotes, the sources for direct and indirect quotations apply in the chapter for which the heading stands. Otherwise, quotations or source references are directly at the word or at the end of the sentence or paragraph. This book contains parts of text based on the Federal Constitution of the Swiss Confederation of 18 April 1999 (as of 12 February 2017), abbreviated to BV[1] and the Constitution of the Canton of Bern of 6 June 1993 (as of 11 March 2015), abbreviated to KV[2] .

If the constitutional paragraph, or individual paragraphs thereof, are based in whole or in part on extracts from the BV or KV, this is indicated in a footnote. The references to the corresponding footnotes for constitutional paragraphs are usually found after the heading of the affected chapter and sometimes in the body of the text. Articles used in the Swiss constitutions are listed in the footnote with a number after the title of the constitutional paragraph. Example: §123 Sample title: BV Art.123, KV Art.123.

All internet sources are fully cited in the footnotes. They were last accessed on 30.09.2021. All literature sources are also listed in full in the footnotes.

All references to tasks undertaken by other ministries and described in more detail there are given in footnotes. Example: Model Ministry - 1.2.3 Model Chapter.

All footnotes are to be viewed in comparison to the respective source, so-called indirect quotations. Direct quotations are set in italics, but hardly ever occur. The source reference is intended to enable further investigation and to take copyright

---

1 This is not an official publication. Only the publication by the Swiss Federal Chancellery is authoritative. https://www.fedlex.admin.ch/eli/cc/1999/404/de On 14.12.2021

2 This is not an official publication. The Bernese Official Collection of Laws is authoritative. https://www.belex.sites.be.ch/frontend/versions/2420?locale=de#ART71 On 16.12.2021

into account.

Table of contents

1 Goals of the Ministry of Foreign Affairs

The aim of the Ministry of Foreign Affairs is to remedy the negative consequences of international anarchy, imperialism and industrialisation in order to subsequently reconcile the world's population in a federal state.

The goals of the Ministry of Foreign Affairs are peace, freedom, protection against exploitation, equitable globalisation, the spread of dynamic media democracy and the empowerment of humanity to govern itself directly democratically. Peace is achieved by the Ministry of Foreign Affairs through peace treaties, freedom through the dismantling of border fortifications and protection against exploitation is ensured through regularisation of guest work, tariffs, import and export restrictions. Equitable globalisation is ensured by an international policy that adapts to the speed of integration of each people. The peoples express their speed of integration through committees and voting on international agreements and quotas of foreign nationals. By obliging states in the dynamic media democracy to involve other affected peoples in their decision-making, these peoples come to know and appreciate the dynamic media democracy. By standardising international measures for communitarisation in an International Union, democratic political structures and processes are introduced at the international level. The aim is to democratise international legislation, jurisprudence, mediation and execution until humanity has the voting right to govern itself collectively.

The aim of embassies and representations abroad is the diplomatic and later democratic negotiation of agreements with foreigners. These agreements serve the purpose of communitarisation and the creation of international law. The aim of communitarisation is world peace and the integration of states towards a single directly democratically controlled state in the world.

The Ministry of Foreign Affairs aims to better protect humanity from natural disasters through an international policy of regional self-sufficiency. Regions or continents are therefore able to support themselves independently with direct goods such as food and medicine, electricity, water and housing. Power plants can also remain switched off in regions as long as the regions on the equator supply solar power, but they must be available for emergencies. If a volcano erupts or the earth shakes, no region should collapse and at worst then create a domino effect because the degree of division of labour between the regions has become so great.

2 Departments

The departments are divided into sub-departments and enumerations are usually considered as their individual units. Many tasks of some departments are completely taken over by other ministries as a service.

2.1 Central Department

Part of the Central Department is the Reception Office with the Courier and Mail Room, which directs all concerns, broadcasts and visitors to the appropriate place in the ministry.

2.1.1 Staff

The Human Resources Department is responsible for staff development and planning. For this purpose, it takes care of recruitment of junior staff, intern and trainee programmes, as well as selection procedures for employees and special selection procedures for applicants with disabilities. For politicians and employees, the department prepares a job plan. In all its tasks, it works in voting with the personnel board.[1]
All other personnel matters are transferred to the relevant ministries. The Ministry of Education is responsible for the training and further education of employees for the state service.[2] The Ministry of Labour takes over the service law.[3] This includes labour and collective bargaining law for employees in the state service, remuneration, personnel

---

1 Ministry of State Organisation - 2.1.1.1 Personnel board
2 Ministry of Education - 2.1.1.1 Education and training for the state service
3 Ministry of Labour - 4 State enterprises, 13 Labour Directory

administration of all careers and employees, flexitime, holiday and sick leave, working time with or without flexitime in part-time or full-time at the place of work or in home work. The Ministry of Infrastructure provides housing assistance for all state employees.[4] The Ministry of Finance's Pay Office takes care of employees' salary, expenses, travel and relocation costs.[5] The Ministry of Education provides childcare for all employees in the state service.[6]

The Ministry of Health is responsible for the occupational health service.[7] It ensures occupational health management, deals with the treatment, education and prevention of occupational accidents, controls and provides occupational health and safety through the health auditors[8] of the Company Auditing Agency[9] .

2.1.2 Organisation

The ministries of media, security, justice, finance, labour, state organisation provide audit services for quality management in the ministry, evaluation of work performance, revenues and expenditures, as well as prevention of corruption, protection against sabotage and, if necessary, disciplinary matters.[10]

The Ministry of Labour regulates procurement law and ensures corruption-free state orders and procurement.[11] The Ministry of Finance organises the annual budget vote and ensures proper accounting in each ministry.[12] It regulates budget procedures, budget law, staff budgets, departmental budgets, costs and cash management, and assists ministries in budget planning for the budget vote. The language service for translating talks or texts is provided by the Ministry of

---

4 Ministry of Infrastructure - 2.1.1.1 Housing assistance for state service employees
5 Ministry of Finance - 2.1.1.1 Staff remuneration
6 Ministry of Education - 2.1.1.2 Childcare for state service employees
7 Ministry of Health - 2.1.1.1 Occupational Health Service
8 Ministry of Labour - 20.7.2 Health auditor
9 Ministry of Labour - 20 Company Auditing Agency
10 Ministries of Media, Security, Justice, Finance, State Organisation - 2.1.2.1 Audit services
11 Ministry of Labour - 6 Procurement Office
12 Ministry of Finance - 8 state revenues, 9 state expenditure

Education.[13]

The Ministry of Digital Affairs supports the supply of Information Technology.[14] In voting with the Procurement Office of the Ministry of Labour, it takes care of the procurement, provision, maintenance and service of technical devices and software. Much of this is produced in-house to ensure data protection in information and communication technology. Information technology and digitalisation officers audit and advise the ministries. Digital appointment calendar and documentation services are provided as well as a digital policy archive including a library.

2.2 Management Department

The Management Department is the minister's department. With his office team, he provides policy planning and analysis for his ministry and coordinates the relationship between the nation and the municipality through exchanges with his deputies in the municipalities. He initiates cooperation with other ministries or citizens in committees and is supported by the Ministry of State Organisation.

The Ministry of Media Affairs, through its media service, provides press and public relations for the ministry, moderates civil dialogue, trains or provides a spokesperson for the minister, writes speeches and texts on request, and ensures the implementation of conferences and events.[15]

The Ministry of Digital Affairs is responsible for digital management and thus provides departmental management. It automatically produces business statistics, staff surveys and the current state of research through statistics. It automatically forwards proposals to the affected or empowered state employees. In document management, it ensures digitalisation and that ministries share forms with each other.[16]

---

13 Ministry of Education - 2.1.3 Language Service
14 Ministry of Digital Affairs - 2.1.2.1.1 Supply of Information Technology
15 Ministry of Media Affairs - 2.2.1.1 Media Service
16 Ministry of Digital Affairs - 2.1.2.1 Digital Service

2.3 Foreign Department

The Foreign Department is responsible for the rules of foreign affairs and communitarisation and their implementation by domestic citizens ministries. It oversees the Foreign Office, embassies, representations and operates the Travel Directory[17] . In cooperation with the Ministry of Education, it operates the Institutes for Peace and Conflict Studies and Communitarisation. It coordinates their cooperation with other ministries and the Minister of Foreign Affairs. It drafts laws on the basics of negotiating international treaties, supranational laws in diplomatic and democratic negotiations, and on the structure and procedures in an International Union.

2.4 International Department

The International Department is responsible for ensuring that ministries comply with international law. If necessary, draft amendments are developed with the foreign minister and forwarded to the embassies or representations. The International Department oversees the democratisation of international law and the handling of international law by the ministries. It exchanges information with all embassies and representations in order to report regularly to the Minister for Foreign Affairs. It prepares templates for the bases of communitarisation and unification of states on continents and around the world. This includes the handling of the institutions of the United Nations and other international organisations or intergovernmental agreements. The individual ministries submit their templates for international policies to the International Department, which forwards them to the appropriate representation to the international organisation or to the embassies in the affected countries.
The staff ensures that all foreign affairs developments in the policy sections of all ministries from all over the world are compiled and summarised by the embassies. At regular intervals, they are forwarded by the Foreign Office to the

---

17 Ministry of Digital Affairs - 12 Directories

responsible ministries. If ministries wish to contact the foreign ministries, the Foreign Office establishes contact through its embassies.

2.5 Development Department

The Development Department ensures cooperation with the ministries of infrastructure, education, labour, health, digital and integration for development aid and asylum application procedures. It runs the Institute for Development Aid and oversees its own, continental and international aid. It recruits and supervises development workers. In the event of a disaster, it sets up a temporary working group. It prepares draft legislation for the Minister of Foreign Affairs and oversees compliance with the rules of its own, continental and international development policy. It coordinates cooperation between the embassies and the Integration Agency in asylum procedures. When voting takes place in a developing country, the Development Department works with the ministries of state organisation, education, media and digital affairs to set up and oversee procedures.

3 Tasks of the Ministry of Foreign Affairs

The Ministry of Foreign Affairs is responsible for all foreign affairs. For this purpose, it maintains authorities that enable the state to act internationally. All international negotiations of the state must be democratically approved by the people. The Minister of Foreign Affairs is responsible for this. The main task of the Ministry of Foreign Affairs is the democratic communitarisation of law and ministries on the continents and throughout the world. The task is considered fulfilled when the states unify until only one state remains.

The Ministry of Foreign Affairs fulfils the task of building an International Union and democratising the United Nations in the sense of an International Union, both in terms of structures and processes as well as in the previously communitarised policy areas. The task is fulfilled as soon as all continental states unify and later all states worldwide. The Ministry of

Foreign Affairs supports other states in communitarisation on their continent.

The Ministry of Foreign Affairs ensures that international law can be applied in the ministries and can be democratically voted down and renewed by the people. Together with all responsible ministries, influence is exerted on continental or international policy areas.

Peacekeeping is a task that the Ministry of Foreign Affairs fulfils by concluding peace treaties with as many states as possible. In this way, the Ministry of Foreign Affairs also ensures a worldwide reduction in military costs.

Development aid is also a task of the Ministry of Foreign Affairs. It identifies unsafe countries of origin and developing countries and supports them with aid. Development aid begins inland and works its way through neighbouring countries to all affected member states on the continent. International development aid is limited to emergency humanitarian aid. Continental development aid increasingly develops a neighbouring underdeveloped continent.

The Ministry of Foreign Affairs has the task of enabling affected humans to apply for asylum. In its embassies, it ensures the safe processing of the asylum application procedure through local knowledge. In doing so, it receives requirements from the Ministry of Integration regarding existing capacities inland.

Ultimately, the Ministry of Foreign Affairs has the task of abolishing itself. This is due to the fact that development aid and asylum provide help for self-help, which makes further aid unnecessary afterwards. Through communitarisation, there are fewer foreign ministries because the number of states is reduced, until eventually there are no more foreigners.

4 Foreign affairs[18]

The Ministry of Foreign Affairs is responsible for foreign affairs. These are communitarisation, continental policy, international policy, development aid and asylum, as well as all concerns of other ministries with foreign countries. The Ministry of Foreign Affairs maintains the Foreign Office,

18§162,1 Foreign affairs: BV Art.54, §166,1 Relations with foreigners and international law treaties: BV Art.166, §163,1,4 Relations with

which is responsible for domestic cooperation with ministries and municipalities. Abroad, the Ministry of Foreign Affairs maintains embassies which ensure cooperation with the state and its responsible offices. Unlike the other ministries, the Ministry of Foreign Affairs does not have offices in town halls. The deputy foreign ministers are the ambassadors and representatives who are directly elected. The Foreign Office has its headquarters in the capital city of the Ministry of Foreign Affairs. It maintains groups of negotiators as diplomats who specialise in negotiations for the various ministries' remits and foreign affairs.

The Minister of Foreign Affairs is responsible for involving the people in international treaties or supranational laws agreed between the inland and foreign countries. The rights of participation include all voting rights that also apply to legislation, whether international treaties or supranational laws. These are namely the veto quorum, the repeal quorum or the counter-proposal.[19] In order to be able to exercise these rights appropriately, all international treaties and supranational laws are filmed and broadcast on government television .[20]

4.1 International treaties[21]

International treaties are all treaties between the state and another state or foreigner company. International treaties do not have a monopoly on the use of force to guarantee them, so they are not laws. International treaties regulate the responsibilities of security agencies and courts. In some cases, responsibilities are assigned to a country, shared, or security agencies or courts are created specifically to oversee compliance with the treaty. Peoples with whose state or company an international treaty is concluded must at least vote on the negotiated treaty text before it becomes valid. For this to happen, 65% of those entitled to vote must be in

foreigners: BV Art.184
19Ministry of State Organisation - 9.10.4 Counter-proposal, 9.5.14 Veto quorum, 9.5.15 Repeal quorum
20Ministry of Media Affairs - 7 Government Television, 7.2.2 Filming of laws
21§163.4 Relations with foreigners

favour. If the foreign minister so requests, his or her people are also involved in the negotiation of the treaty text.

The Minister of Foreign Affairs is responsible for signing international treaties after the ministries involved have given their approval and a majority of the affected peoples have expressed their support. As a result of the treaties, amendments to laws or bills may become necessary. The Foreign Office is responsible for initiating and supervising this process of ratification, i.e. incorporation into national law, at the ministry responsible.

The Minister of Foreign Affairs may issue regulations that bring about the immediate implementation of international agreements that have already been approved by a majority of the affected peoples. These regulations are limited in time until the responsible ministry submits a corresponding law and the people agree to it by a majority. Regulations are only permissible if it is in the interest of the country to bring about immediate implementation.

4.2 Supranational laws

Supranational laws are requirements that have arisen in an International Union. All member states of this International Union agree on requirements and have a common jurisdiction for their International Union. Supranational laws can only arise in communitarised ministries that are in the middle ring of International Union integration. They become national laws as soon as the member states move into the inner ring and establish a federal state. In an International Union, all peoples always have a right of co-determination that corresponds to that of the legislative process, as do the majority ratios.[22]

---

[22] Ministry of State Organisation - 9.10.11 Three Ways of Legislation

4.3 Diplomatic negotiations

At the international level, anarchy still prevails, i.e. the law of the militarily strongest. The aim of this ministry is to change that. At the international level, diplomatic conditions predominate. Negotiations that have to be conducted diplomatically, i.e. in secret, can more easily cost the Foreign Minister his office. All other ministers can call votes or committees. The Foreign Minister can only ask foreign negotiators to conduct the negotiations in public with him or ask other peoples to vote.

The Ministry of Foreign Affairs, with its diplomats, is responsible for conducting international negotiations and caring for international relations that are not conducted within the framework of the International Union. All foreigners working inland are regularly invited to events for the Diplomatic Corps to get to know each other better.

The diplomats of the Ministry of Foreign Affairs conduct diplomatic negotiations mainly at international conferences, intergovernmental events and summits. All diplomats involved adhere to the Vienna Convention on Diplomatic Relations. It contains rules on the negotiating methods, accreditation and immunity of diplomats.[23]

Diplomatic negotiations are secret and conducted by diplomats. If politicians conduct diplomatic negotiations, the people can obtain disclosure or participation through a veto quorum. The foreign minister is liable for all the secret results of negotiations. Decisions made diplomatically only become effective when the majority of the affected population has agreed. This applies to both the own and the other population. If the government of the affected country does not want to hold a referendum, its own population can accept or reject the diplomatic decision. Diplomatic decisions that are to lead to communitarisation must be subject to direct democratic voting by the peoples involved.

---

[23] https://www.admin.ch/opc/de/classified-compilation/19610070/index.html

4.3.1 Diplomats

Diplomats have a duty to behave diplomatically in negotiations. This means that they must be willing to compromise, recognise the intentions and wishes of the negotiating partners and reconcile them with the intentions and wishes of their own state. This harmony should put each Negotiator in a better position after the negotiations than before. In negotiations, diplomats look for So-called win-win situations that increase the benefits of the negotiating partners for as long as possible. Diplomatic behaviour avoids cornering or exposing other negotiating partners.[24]

Diplomats assume representational duties in the international relations of globalisation. Politicians from the member states take over foreign policy in international unifications. Diplomats support the communication of politicians from different states and federal levels as well as with civil society, which is organised in associations.

Diplomacy connects the international level with the national and municipal levels. Diplomats assume a communication function that informs democratically elected politicians of their mutual interests in such a way that the politicians can agree on legally binding agreements between states or municipalities and cities of different states and have them voted on by the affected peoples or inhabitants of municipalities. Diplomacy promotes internal exchanges between politicians and administers them through diplomats working in several policy remits of several states.[25]

Diplomats are envoys of states to deliver news, namely Foreign Office negotiators and embassy staff. They treat the contents of the news confidentially and, as bearers, are not liable for its content. Therefore, diplomats enjoy immunity worldwide in the course of their diplomatic activities in order to be able to guarantee the delivery of news at all times. Diplomats are becoming less important as communications and Information Technology digitalise the delivery of news.

---

24 https://de.wikipedia.org/wiki/Diplomatie
25 Rausch, Ulrike: Diplomatie, in: Nohlen, Dieter; Schultze, Rainer-Olaf (eds.) 2004: Lexikon der Politikwissenschaft. Theorien, Methoden, Begriffe, C.H.Beck, Munich, p.153, ISBN 3406511260.

Moreover, the territorial state is increasingly disappearing in favour of continental states and eventually a world state. While diplomats work for international unifications, ministers and their deputies are those who work in an International Union. Democratic structures and processes apply in an International Union as integration progresses towards the inner ring. While diplomats still work in the outer ring, they lose their importance in the middle ring as soon as the ministry for whose remit they are responsible becomes communitarised.

4.4 Democratic negotiations[26]

All diplomatic negotiations are democratised in such a way that their treaty text is submitted to the voting of the affected peoples before it can enter into force. The Ministry of Media Affairs is responsible for filming the treaty text and broadcasting it on Government Television. The Ministry of Foreign Affairs strives to conduct as many international negotiations democratically as possible. This means that the negotiation steps correspond to the political processes for legislation. The political processes in an International Union are fundamentally democratic and not diplomatic. The majority proposal prevails and special rules are made for minorities. Unlike diplomats, politicians can be deselected by the people at any time.[27]
Politicians are entitled to request opinions from diplomats, which they can disclose to citizens. Citizens have the right to request opinions from the Minister of Foreign Affairs or to set up a committee, which they can do by means of a veto quorum.[28] If a citizen's personal or professional interests are affected or customs arrangements are made, the Minister of Foreign Affairs must convene a committee. Committees on Customs agreements determine the amount of tariffs and the trade goods to be paid duty on. The people vote on this and

---

26§164 Participation of citizens in foreign policy decisions: BV Art. 55, §165 Relations of the municipalities with foreign countries: BV Art. 56, §152,5 Tariffs
27Ministry of State Organisation - 9.5.10 Deselection quorum
28Ministry of State Organisation - 9.6 Committee, 9.5.14 Veto quorum

can change the level of tariffs as part of the budget vote .[29] Municipalities can conclude international treaties with other foreigner municipalities through democratic negotiations if they administer the necessary responsibility for this on a municipal level.[30] The Ministry of Media Affairs must also film these inter-municipal treaties and broadcast them on Government Television. The people can prevent the citizens of a municipality from concluding a treaty through a veto quorum if the treaty would be contrary to national laws or the common good of the people. Municipalities may cooperate with offices of other states and must regularly inform the citizens about this cooperation. The Ministry of Media Affairs is responsible for preparing the information in videos and texts and publishing it on Party Television[31] and on the intranet. This allows citizens to trigger the veto quorum in case of doubt in order to involve themselves or the foreign minister in the cooperation.

Democratic negotiations are public and are not necessarily conducted by elected politicians with elected persons. At any time during the negotiation process, the population has the possibility to stop or change the negotiations. This happens when a quorum of 30% of the population triggers a voting. The question to be asked is: "Should the negotiations continue, be democratised or broken off?" The answer options by cross are: "continue __ democratise __ break off __". In diplomatic negotiations, democratising means that an elected person should lead the negotiations. In democratic negotiations, the negotiations must then continue as a show on Government Television with audience participation.[32] Negotiations are conducted by several elected moderators[33] and one or more elected politicians in a public debate.[34]

The population can demand more democratic political processes through a quorum. In the Ministry of Foreign Affairs,

---

29 Ministry of Finance - 9.5 Budget vote
30 Ministry of State Organisation - 10.3 Subsidiarity vote
31 Ministry of Media - 10 Party Television
32 Ministry of Media Affairs - 7.2.3.5 Solution Finder (Legislation Committee)
33 Ministry of State Organisation - 4.4.3 Federal Moderators
34 Ministry of State Organisation - 9.6 Committee

this applies, for example, to aid deliveries, trade agreements or treaties on continental integration.

4.5 Speed of integration

The dissolution of boundaries through globalisation must match its speed to the speed of integration of the humans of different cultures and regions. Peoples and municipalities express their speed of integration in committees and voting on international agreements and quotas of foreign nationals.[35] Governments base their actions on this. In the process, the speed of immigration and communitarisation is adapted to the population with the slowest speed of integration, because otherwise these humans will feel left behind and rebel.

Many states used national consciousness to create a kind of family cohesion among their population. The aim is to replace this with constitutional patriotism. It is developed out of joy in the society in which one lives, because one is proud of the rules set together for peaceful coexistence as a people.

In the past, many flags displayed many banners of the powerful. Flags are interchangeable and will disappear from consciousness after generations have passed unless they last the centuries in cultural protection areas. In this way, it is possible to dismantle borders over about 10 generations until a networks of direct democracy spans the earth to regulate and control the real and digital traffic of living beings, goods and information for the benefit of all. Administrative costs will be reduced and all humans will unite their forces to quickly and cheaply find space on other planets before life on Earth is no longer possible. The goal is to ensure the survival of humanity through a family life with 1 to 3 children, whereby the generation sequence can be shortened or extended.

---

35 Ministry of Integration - 7.4 Quota of foreigners

4.6 Foreign Office

All domestic services that the Ministry of Foreign Affairs provides for other ministries are handled by the Foreign Office. This office also coordinates the state's geostrategic decisions and votes on them with the domestic population.

The Foreign Office has the best negotiators in the country. They all make the appointments that ambassadors make when it comes to concluding political or economic agreements. The negotiators specialise in communitarisation through diplomacy and democracy, as well as in one of the topics of continental policy, international policy, development aid, asylum or a ministry's remit. Negotiators are suitably matched to negotiate strategic foreign projects.

The Foreign Office oversees the travel and visit programmes of domestic diplomats and politicians to foreign countries as well as foreign diplomats and politicians coming to the inland. Visits by heads of state, heads of government and foreign ministers are governed by an international protocol organised by Foreign Office staff. The protocol includes the hosting of diplomatic and consular visitors and includes social events in function rooms of the responsible ministries and assistance at airports. Travel conditions can be comfortable or easy, depending on how much money the people allocate to the Foreign Office in the budget vote for this service provision.[36]

During domestic visits, personnel status issues are clarified for all fellow travellers in order to be able to issue visas for the duration of stay, protocol passes for the area of responsibility and accreditations for the events.

4.7 Embassies

The Ministry of Foreign Affairs maintains an embassy in every country in the world as a diplomatic or democratic representation. There is no embassy in countries that refuse to do so. As a matter of principle, the Ministry of Foreign Affairs does not refuse to maintain an embassy in a country. Even if relations with a country are broken off as a punitive measure,

---

36Ministry of Finance - 9.5 Budget vote

the embassy remains as a peace offering to resume negotiations. Only if the lives of the embassy staff are threatened is the embassy closed. The government of the affected country is invited to contact the Minister of Foreign Affairs at any time to resume peaceful relations. It maintains a representation for each international unification and International Union. Representations are not called embassies because they do not serve states.

When own diplomats and politicians visit a foreign country or an international unification or union, all fellow travellers are looked after by the embassy. The support includes accommodation, meals, transport and staff status issues. Depending on the staff status during the visits, appropriate visas for the duration of the stay, protocol passes for the area of responsibility and accreditations for the events are organised. Ambassadors are politicians directly elected by the people from the foreign party. Their new election can additionally be obtained by a quorum of the domestic population. For this purpose, 60% of the domestic population must express their wish for the deselection of the incumbent ambassador with their passport at the embassy or one of its consulates. In the case of representations to an international club or unification, a majority of 60% of all the peoples of the states involved is required.

Embassies are not connected to the intranet because it would be too risky to be spied on or infected here. The data is transmitted in encrypted form via satellite or the Internet and fed into the intranet or output by the Ministry of Digital Affairs.

4.7.1 Representations to international organisations

Representations to international organisations are not considered embassies because they do not work for a sovereign state but for an international organisation. They establish contacts between domestic and foreign ministries, companies and international organisations. International organisations, such as the United Nations, G20 or OECD, conclude treaties. During the initiation, negotiation, signing and review of the implementation of international treaties, the representations support and advise the domestic contractual partners. In particular, when the Foreign Office sends negotiators, the representation informs them about the current status of the international organisation and supports them in the negotiations.

4.7.2 Representations to International Unions

The representations to the International Union coordinate the communitarisation of all member states. In individual groups, all ministries that are communitarised are looked after. In cooperation with the embassies for the countries, the ministries of the member state are looked after. In cooperation with the Foreign Office, the domestic ministries are looked after. The Representation is responsible for briefing Foreign Office negotiators and assisting them in negotiations. It thus takes over the task of the Federal Moderator's Office[37] , in order to ensure supranational political processes in the structures of the International Union.

The representations to the global Union, i.e. the United Nations, and the representation to the Continental Union, i.e. the Continental Union, coordinate their voting. The representations make sure that responsibilities are clearly separated by remit so that voters can easily identify the responsible politician.

4.7.3 Embassies for countries[38]

Embassies for countries have the task of maintaining child support for the politicians there. This enables intergovernmental agreements to be concluded. Embassy staff are responsible for looking after the various departments of the Ministry of

37 Ministry of State Organisation - 4.4 Federal Moderator's Office
38 §24 Protection against expulsion, extradition and deportation: BV Art.25

Foreign Affairs. Depending on whether a country is affected by communitarisation, asylum or development aid, there are more or fewer staff members with the necessary qualifications in the embassy.

The embassy in a developing country manages development aid when it is the developing country's turn. The embassies of unsafe countries of origin are responsible for asylum application procedures in cooperation with other embassies of safe neighbouring countries.

Embassies for countries may also operate consulates in the country. Depending on the size of the country or the workload of the embassy, consulates are established or closed.

The embassies for countries support the Ministry of Security in Tax Investigation, extradition requests and deportations. In the case of a Tax Investigation Department, the embassy asks the country's Finance Minister for access to certain financial data of companies. For extradition requests, the embassy asks the country's security minister to hand over wanted criminals at the country's border or to allow its own security forces to search the Country-of-destination. Extradition requests from abroad are granted if the person is a national of that country, is a foreigner, does not enjoy asylum and has not committed a criminal offence in the inland. Nationals will only be extradited if the person affected agrees or if a domestic court orders it by means of a judgement.

The embassy negotiates with the integration minister of the foreign country about the permission and the time limit for entries from this country into the inland as well as from the inland into this foreign country.

4.7.3.1 Consulates

Consulates are responsible for individual relationship areas such as trade, production and value chains. Domestic entrepreneurs who wish to establish child support with companies abroad can do so through the consulate. The consulate then profiles the foreigner companies in the Labour Directory to link their economic activity with the profiles of domestic citizens in the Labour Directory. As part of the regular audits, the consulate works with auditors from the Company Auditing Agency. The consulate educates domestic citizens about the costs incurred by the examinations and what can happen if there are deficiencies. After some time, consulates become familiar with foreign companies and their audit results. Companies with multiple deficiencies can be excluded from all foreign trade or only from certain economic forms. The embassy is responsible for the exclusion in voting with the consul.

4.7.3.2 Stay abroad[39]

Those who are nationals living abroad on a permanent basis are considered foreigners. They can establish contact with each other through the embassy in the country or their consulates if there is mutual consent. Nationals living abroad are not entitled to use the People's Computer[40] and the intranet abroad. They lose their political voting rights, the right to social benefits and the obligation to perform People's Service for one year. As soon as nationals living abroad or their descendants return home and live inland, they regain their full rights as citizens.

4.7.3.3 Help abroad

Domestic nationals who are abroad can receive assistance at the embassy or their consulates. Assistance includes passport replacement in the event of loss or theft, legal assistance for foreign laws in the event of damage, financial assistance in emergencies, home tours, evacuations, search for missing relatives and assistance with the repatriation of deceased relatives. The embassy can alert its own security forces for assistance, or security forces of the respective foreigner. The embassy's own security forces may only be armed with the

---

39 §42 Nationals living abroad: BV Art.40
40 Ministry of Digital Affairs - 13.6 People's Computers

consent of the foreign government.

4.7.3.4 Visa[41]

Visas are required by nationals wishing to travel abroad and by foreigners wishing to enter inland. Nationals of countries with which visa-free travel has been agreed are exempt. Such an agreement can be reached if the standard of living is the same in both countries or if they are in an International Union. The embassies issue visas to foreigners seeking entry if they are not criminals or in debt. The Ministry of Integration issues the laws on immigration[42] , to which the embassy adheres and only issues appropriate visas. A visa expires automatically if the holder commits a criminal offence while staying inland. Special visas are available for guest workers and asylum seekers.

4.7.3.5 Guest work

Nationals who wish to work abroad as guest workers can apply for a temporary or permanent work visa through the embassy of the desired foreign country and send the police clearance certificates.
For work visas of foreigners, the embassy abroad grants or denies permission for guest work. Embassy staff in the respective foreign country obtain police clearance certificates on the applicants from the responsible authorities abroad. This cooperation is coordinated and carried out with the Ministry of Labour.[43]

4.7.3.6 Deportations[44]

The embassy ensures the unproblematic deportation of its own nationals from abroad to the inland. Refusal of repatriation is not permitted. In the case of deportations of offenders,

41 §243.1 Legislation on foreigners and asylum: BV Art. 121
42 Ministry of Integration - Immigration
43 Ministry of Labour - 16.11 Guest work
44 §162,6 Foreign affairs: BV Art. 54, §243,1,3-5 Legislation on foreigners and asylum: BV Art. 121

all investigation files and evidence must be handed over to the embassy of the Country-of-destination. The embassy sends the data to the Ministry of Justice. Criminals who are deported are picked up directly at the border by Customs and taken into custody, where they face a proper charge in court. Customs and the Integration Agency take care of the deportations.[45] The embassy contacts the country of origin of those to be deported. If foreigners are to be deported, embassy staff inform the local authorities. If admission of the nationals is refused, negotiators from the Foreign Office enter into negotiations. They are able to initiate all peaceful punitive measures, such as trade restrictions, economic embargoes, entry bans and account seizures. The punitive measures and their deadlines must be approved by the Foreign Minister.
The Ministry of Security is responsible for the safe transport of the deportees to the country of origin. The journey is only accompanied diplomatically by the embassy staff.

4.7.3.7 War

In the event of war, the embassy is vacated and all staff evacuated to their homeland. The ambassadors continue their activities from the headquarters in the capital city and conduct peace negotiations. The Ministry of Security takes over the war operations against the country.[46]

4.8 Travel Directory

In the Travel Directory, each profile consists of all entries and departures of a person. In the case of nationals, the profile is stored in the Persons Directory[47] and the travel data is stored on the People's Computer[48] . Foreigners entering and leaving the country receive a profile in the Travel Directory when they first enter the country, in which their date of departure is stored.

---

45 Ministry of Security - 8.2.8 Departure of persons, Ministry of Integration - 7.9 Departure procedures
46 Ministry of Security - 9.5 Warfare
47 Ministry of State Organisation - 4.6 Persons Directory
48 Ministry of Digital Affairs - 13.6 People's Computers

In this way, the Ministry of Foreign Affairs always knows which foreigners are inland and which domestic citizens are abroad. The Travel Directory is used to check compliance with the quota of foreigners[49] as well as deadlines for visas and residence permits.

Persons travelling together can form a travel group. Tour operators can make information and voting available to their travellers in the travel group via the Travel Directory.

4.9 Institute for Peace and Conflict Research

The Institute for Peace and Conflict Research advises the Ministry of Foreign Affairs and carries out its research assignments. Institutes of the universities can be called upon by the Ministry of Foreign Affairs to collaborate. In addition to the ambassadors from the field, academics familiar with the theory are also consulted to provide assessments. Institutes may also approach this contact point in the Ministry of Foreign Affairs if they think they can provide useful information. The aim is to be able to better assess international moods, inter-state tensions and national situations. The data on peacemaking and conflict situations are used to formulate laws or to achieve the intended purpose with the available means. The long-term purpose is to create peace between humans and to resolve conflicts peacefully. After the end of the Ministry of Foreign Affairs, the Institute for Peace and Conflict Research will move to the Ministry of Integration, where it helps to reduce tensions between cultural protection areas.

5 Communitarisation[50]

Communitarisation means the linking of peoples through diplomacy, such as in the UN, and through democracy, such as in the Continental Union. Through diplomats, peace treaties and free trade agreements are negotiated and voted on by the peoples involved. Through international politicians and the peoples affected, a world language is developed and

49 Ministry of Integration - 7.4 Quota of foreigners
50 §168,2-4,7 World peace: BV Art. 121, §163,2,3,4 Relations with foreigners: BV Art.184

consultations are held as citizens' consultations or committees. Communitarisation refers to any cooperation based on treaty, law or constitution. While international treaties are mainly negotiated diplomatically, international laws and constitutions of new federal states must be determined democratically. International treaties that serve communitarisation must be voted on with those affected and must be supported by over 65% of those entitled to vote. If another people is not entitled to vote, the responsible minister of that people assumes the voting right. The people can vote for or against the participation of the other people and otherwise reject the treaty.

Communitarisation aims to guarantee the independence and military neutrality of individual states and federal states. At the same time, countries are increasingly networking through international unifications and membership in an International Union. Communitarisation aims to avoid war or keep it as short and painless as possible.

5.1 Goals of communitarisation

The aim of communitarisation is to accompany humans on the path to a world constitution. The path is the goal, because at the end of this path it is achieved that all humans experience their existence on earth in the same state and regulate themselves democratically.

Communitarisation is being pursued in regions and worldwide at the same time. The aim of continental politics is the democratic communitarisation of existing political structures and processes up to the unification of all member states in the United States of the Continent. The same goal applies to the united states of Europe, America, Africa, Arapersia and Asia.

At the same time, international policy aims to standardise rules and standards worldwide so that the same law applies to all humans everywhere. Exceptions to the protection of minorities are permitted in individual municipalities, but not changes to the constitution. The aim is to overcome borders wherever they are unnecessary and to create borders where niches are necessary. Development aid is used to support communitarisation in order to standardise living standards worldwide. Asylum offers temporary protection in emergency situations and works together with the humanitarian aid of the unified nations.

In the course of communitarisation, global ministries replace national or continental ministries and reduce the number of ministers and their state apparatus. The goal is for more and more humans to be governed by fewer and fewer politicians, until only 17 ministers remain worldwide, each with a deputy in every municipality in the world. Accordingly, the Ministry of Foreign Affairs aims to abolish itself.

5.2 Procedure of communitarisation

The task of communitarisation is to standardise the rules for living together and to reduce the number of states. Negotiations on communitarisation use the model of dynamic media democracy to involve citizens appropriately. The International Union is the model of how states can become federal states democratically and without war. The Continental Union is the International Union of the continent. The states of the other continents also each found an International Union. As soon as all member states of an International Union have united to form a federal state, a continental Union is ready to communitarise with another continental Union. Once all continental International Unions have communitarised, the goal of a united states of the world is achieved and communitarisation is complete.

To this end, communitarisation is also used in development aid and asylum policy. Textbooks are written and films made on how to introduce dynamic media democracy on a municipal, national and global scale. Any willing population can access this knowledge free of charge and in the national language.

If there is not yet a translation in that language, interpreters from the responsible embassy will make a translation.

If a power vacuum arises because a revolution has successfully degraded a despot, a political structure including political processes can be built with the help of dynamic media democracy to find the will of the people and transform it into a constitution. The more similar the constitutions of the states in the world become, the better communitarisation can succeed. The speed of integration of the affected peoples determines the duration of communitarisation.

5.3 Peace treaties[51]

The Ministry of Foreign Affairs concludes peace treaties with as many states as possible. Increased efforts shall be made in the short term for peace treaties with the economically strongest states and neighbouring states. Peace treaties should be obligatory within and between International Unions and unified states. A war between two unified states would endanger humanity and the earth and must be prevented at all costs. In the event of hardening of the fronts of discussion, it should be possible to separate them by drawing fortified borders, so that both opposing ways of life can be practised on their territory side by side instead of with each other. Diplomatic and democratic negotiations should take place on a regular basis in order to avoid hereditary enmity and to dare communitarisation again in new generations.

5.4 Free trade agreement[52]

The ministries of Social Market Economy[53] and Free Market Economy[54] have the right to conclude free trade agreements with other states and the duty to involve the people in the

---

51 §168.7 World peace: BV Art. 173, §166.3 Relations with foreigners and treaties under international law
52 §162.4 Foreign affairs, §223.2 Weapons and war material: BV Art. 107
53 Ministry of Social Market Economy
54 Ministry of Free Market Economy

drafting process by means of a committee[55] . Arms exports are only allowed to countries with which an International Union exists. All agreements are subject to democratic voting by all affected peoples. It is not sufficient for only one's own population to have the right to vote directly. As soon as no majority is reached in a state, the agreement with that country does not enter into force.

Direct free trade agreements may only be concluded by the Free Market Economy. For FTAs in the other three economic forms, the affected states or economic forms must either meet the same standards, or democratically agree higher standards with the affected persons of all affected states and economic forms. The standards for goods, services and managing directors are certified by the auditors of the Company Auditing Agency for a fee. Foreign companies that do not wish to trade only with the Free Market Economy must engage the responsible auditors of the Company Auditing Agency for the respective certification as well as pay the travel expenses for the auditors and the fees for the audit.

Free trade agreements with developing countries can only be concluded if the volume of trade is balanced. Imports from the domestic market to the developing country must be equal to the developing country's exports to the domestic market. Neither imports into the inland nor exports from the inland may weaken the economic power in the developing country.

5.5 Consultations

Consultations are questionnaires for all beginning discussions on international treaties, whether with companies or in the context of an International Union, or intergovernmental treaties with third countries. In the Continental Union, consultations are also used for continental legislation.[56] After the first round of negotiations between international politicians, consultations are published in the Legislative Directory[57] and can be filled in by citizens. Each consultation has a period of 4

---

55 Ministry of State Organisation - 9.6 Committee
56 https://ec.europa.eu/info/consultations_de
57 Ministry of State Organisation - 9.10.6.1 Legislative Directory

weeks. After that, the negotiations continue. As all rounds of negotiations are shown publicly on Government Television[58] , citizens can cast their vote for the veto quorum at any time and negotiate the international treaty in a committee.

5.6 Institute for Communitarisation

The Institute for Communitarisation researches the global degree of communitarisation in all international organisations and intergovernmental treaties. All continental and international agreements and institutions are categorised into the three rings of integration. The development of legislative alignment, democratisation, economic development and living standards are examined. The Institute's aim is to find out which states are how well suited for an International Union and what would still need to be done before they are perfectly suited. The Institute receives its data from embassies and representations around the world. The authorities of the Ministry of Foreign Affairs can send research assignments to the Institute to prepare or follow up on their work.

5.7 Theory of state communitarisation

The communitarisation of states serves the purpose of world peace and the life of humanity in harmony with nature and the universe. Harmony with the universe accepts the transience of planet Earth, seeks and colonises habitable planets without exploiting them ruinously. Harmony with nature protects animal and plant species from extinction at the hands of humans and ensures a regenerative burden. World peace requires a development in the minds as well as an alignment or compatibility of the laws and cultural rules of the humans.

---

58 Ministry of Media Affairs - 7.2.3.7 Consultations

5.7.1 Decoupling law and culture

State communitarisation decouples the law and cultural rules of humanity from each other in order to communitarise them with a time lag. For this purpose, International Unions are formed, which in the first step are limited to a coherent cultural area that is as similar as possible and has the same legal history as far as possible. Since before state laws and the state monopoly on the use of force, humans lived primarily according to the requirements of religions, religious attitudes still shape the laws of states today. From the dawn of mankind, tribes and clans gave each other their locally limited rules. Therefore, state communitarisation must respect world religions and continental habits in each region in order to be successful. Respect finds its application in that the boundaries of an International Union are fixed from the outset. The boundaries run along the imprint of religion, language and traditions on the laws. The decisive factor is that state borders are easier and quicker to move or dismantle, or legal standards easier to unify, than religious beliefs, mother tongues and habits that have grown into traditions over generations.

5.7.2 Inheritance of the territorial states

In the age of the territorial state, national borders unified religion, language and traditions in the respective states. In the age of globalisation, the mobility of humanity and money causes migratory movements that break up, question or dismantle unified habits. This creates fear of loss among humans who like to care for these habits, which expresses itself in hatred towards the foreign and unfamiliar. This fact endangers the state communitarisation.

There are two ways around this danger. The first option is to communitarise the state so slowly that, over generations, national borders, laws, religion, languages and traditions converge until national borders lose their meaning. The danger of war is posed by communitarisation that is too fast and the speed of integration of the affected citizens too slow. Wars slow down communitarisation.

5.7.3 Communitarisation of laws in culturally similar areas

The second possibility is to separate laws and national borders from religion, language and tradition and to communitarise the former in a shorter period of time than the latter. The second option is sought by International Unions.

First, the boundaries of an International Union are based on religion, scripture, appearance and behaviour. For example, the Continental Union is limited to Christian values, Latin or Greek characters, fair skin types and behaviour adapted to changing seasons. Therefore, its area of influence stretches from Portugal to Russia and ends roughly at the 45th parallel and the Mediterranean Sea. Secondly, within the International Union, regions for different religions and languages are demarcated by municipalities and cultural protection areas. National borders lose their legal significance when the same law applies on both sides of the border.

Initially, the changeover takes place through diplomatic treaties, which each country translates into laws that suit itself. Later, common laws are agreed and implemented by individual jointly elected politicians who run for election with appropriate programmes. Finally, all ministries and agencies of all member states are governed by ministers directly elected by the people of the International Union.

5.8 International Union[59]

An International Union comes into being whenever at least two states adopt common laws for at least one ministry. The formation of an International Union is undertaken by the foreign ministries of all voluntary states in the continental expansion area. Voluntariness is guaranteed with a majority among the people of at least 60%. The continental expansion area is based on the religious, linguistic and traditional

---

59 §163.5 Relations with foreign countries

character of the local population and is queried at the same time during the voting on accession. The boundaries of the International Union are determined by the entire population of the International Union together with the states of the neighbouring continents and, if necessary, with all the states of the world.

The International Union consists of three So-called rings of political integration towards the centre. Political integration means aligning the laws and constitutional articles between states so that the same law applies everywhere. Political integration becomes democratic when the affected peoples continuously vote on intergovernmental agreements. Rejections despite negotiation in a committee signal a too low speed of integration in the population and a too high presented speed of integration of the International Union. A voting on the same content may be newly held as soon as the associated quorum of 60% of those entitled to vote is fulfilled. Provided that a people meets a quorum of 30%, any negotiation or outcome of negotiations must be negotiated directly democratically in a committee in which the citizens of all affected peoples are entitled to vote.

The establishment of an International Union also includes the establishment of a Union institution for international state organisation, which enables supranational democratised decision-making. The Union institution replaces the Ministry of State Organisation in the outer and middle ring as long as it is not communitarised. The embassies, Foreign Offices and Federal Moderator's Offices[60] of all member states provide the necessary staff, who work in the premises of the Ministries of Foreign Affairs and State Organisation. Once communitarised, the Ministry of State Organisation takes over all the functions of the institution.

5.8.1 Union institution

The Union institution takes over the tasks of the Ministry of State Organisation as long as it is not yet communitarised. This includes which institutions make up the political structures of

---

60 Ministry of State Organisation - 4.4 Federal Moderator's Office

the International Union and how they handle each other in the political processes. It guards the international treaties in which member states regulate their cooperation on the outer and middle ring.[61]

It maintains a moderator's office, whose moderators are the point of contact for citizens and politicians from the member states regarding questions, complaints and suggestions about the responsibility of politically active persons in the International Union. All appointed or elected diplomats or politicians of the member states are politically active in the International Union.[62]

The President of the IU works mainly with the Heads of State or Government or the Foreign Ministers to accompany the transition between rings or the cooperation of several member states in the outer or middle ring. He is directly elected by all the peoples of the International Union member states. Unlike a minister, he cannot make laws, but can only suggest international treaties between member states that regularise political structures and processes on the outer and middle rings. The sovereign member states conclude these treaties after their peoples have given their consent.

To enable reliable cooperation between the Member States, the Union institution cooperates with the Foreign Offices, representations and embassies of the Member States.

5.8.2 Three rings of integration[63]

The External Service is for diplomatic accession, the Middle Service is for the democratic integration of various ministries at different speeds, and the Internal Service is for the establishment of a new federal state with its own constitution. In the outer ring, respect for human rights and a democratic constitution are negotiating conditions, as well as a maximum of 60% of the Gross Domestic Product[64] in national debt. In

---

61 Ministry of State Organisation - 8 Political structure, 9 Political processes, 4.3.1 Guardians of the Constitution
62 Ministry of State Organisation - 4.4 Federal Moderator's Office
63 §162,2,3 Foreign affairs
64 Ministry of Finance - 10.6 Determination of the Gross Domestic Product

the middle ring, all member states have a balanced national budget, no national debt and the same standard of living with the same average real wage per capita. In the inner ring, there is a common direct-democratic constitution, a balanced state budget, savings equal to the budget for the coming year and an equal standard of living. All other minimum standards of the other two rings are maintained.

Any transfer of a member state or one of its ministries between the rings must be approved by a majority of the peoples involved. Any entry into another ring towards the centre is connected to a referendum in all involved member states. The rings have different majorities. To join the outer ring requires a 60% approval in the population, 75% in the middle ring and 90% in the inner ring.

Simultaneous international and continental communitarisation is thus possible. A state can be a member of the outer ring of a continental union and at the same time of the global union. Laws must not contradict each other, authorities must not duplicate each other and responsibilities must not overlap. The voter should be able to keep track of everything. In the middle ring, a state can only communitarise a ministry in an International Union. In the inner ring, states can also only unify in one International Union, not in several International Unions.

5.8.2.1 Outer ring

On the outer ring, treaties between states are formulated diplomatically and voted on by the participating peoples. Every state in the continental area of expansion is automatically a member of the outer ring. In the outer ring, ministries of the various sovereign states work together and adopt common laws or conclude treaties for unification. Not every ministry or member state has to be involved in this. There are possibilities for exceptions, which are negotiated by diplomats or politicians.

All member states of the outer ring conduct international

relations with each other and, on their own initiative, accession negotiations for the middle ring. Accession takes place as soon as the standards of the middle ring are met. The outer ring also serves for states that no longer meet the minimum requirements for the middle ring. They remain in the outer ring until they meet the common laws again.

5.8.2.2 Middle ring[65]

On the middle ring, any number of ministries from different member states are administered together. More and more ministries gradually follow because more and more things are found to be more advantageous as a community in the globalised world.

These international ministries each have a minister who is responsible for the policy remit in all voluntary member states. The international minister is directly elected by the affected peoples and, in voting with those entitled to vote, enacts laws for his or her remit that apply in all member states.

All deputy ministers from the municipalities of the member states shall form the International Council. The same applies to all party wing leaders and delegates from a party from all member states to the International Party Council.[66]

In the middle ring, it is possible that, for example, 3 states jointly administer the Ministry of State Organisation and 9 states administer the Ministry of Labour. Should the Ministry of State Organisation be jointly administered, i.e. communitarised, it can continue to look after nationally administered ministries. A communitarised Ministry of State Organisation only results in the unification of political structures and processes, but not the political contents of the other ministries.

Entry into or exit from an international ministry is possible at any time. The international laws lose their meaning in the withdrawing member state only when they are repealed by the local government or population.

65§102 International Council
66Ministry of State Organisation - 8.6.3 International Council, 8.6.4.3 International Party Council

The international laws apply in the member states as soon as they join the middle ring. This means that if, for example, the Ministries of Labour of two member states are already communitarised in the middle ring and another Ministry of Labour of another member state wants to join, it must adopt the existing laws of the existing two Ministries of Labour.

If a populous country wishes to legislate differently, this intention must be announced before accession, because majority ratios could change afterwards and exits could follow. To avoid such deadlock between member states, it is possible in the middle ring to form up to 2 international unions for the same ministry. For example, there could be 2 international Ministries of Finance if the budget votes are too different. So France, Germany and Poland could run one Ministry of Finance, as well as Spain, Italy and Greece. Whether there is one or two international currencies is left to the member states of all international Ministries of Finance.

5.8.2.3 Inner ring[67]

In the inner ring, member states from the outer and middle ring unite in a federal state with a common constitution. The member states must fulfil certain requirements in order to be able to communitarise in the inner ring. The prerequisites are a uniform standard of living with a similar price level as well as uniform legal and state-organisational conditions. The member states must share national borders, which disappear in the new federal state.

Member states from the outer ring can join the inner ring without going through the middle ring. To do so, they must adopt the constitution in force in the inner ring, run all their ministries accordingly and comply with the laws in force in the inner ring.

Member states from the middle ring are gradually converging their policies and norms. If they wish to join the inner ring, they can propose amendments to the constitution in force in the inner ring. The population of the inner ring then decides

---

67 §55 Communitarisation of States, §102.5 International Council

whether it agrees to a constitutional amendment procedure.[68] If they agree, the constitutional amendment process begins. If they do not agree, the applicant member states can establish another federal state in the middle ring. As a result, in the inner ring with several federal states, there are again three rings of integration to be run-through between these federal states. The aim of the inner ring is to create federal states in order to reduce the number of individual states. If there are several federal states in the inner ring, they communitarise in the same way. First they are on the outer ring as member states with common treaties and laws. Then, in the middle ring, ministries of all member states are brought together in a supranational ministry. Its ministers and politicians are then directly elected by the citizens of all member states. Until finally the constitutions are aligned. This process is repeated until there is only one federal state on each continent and then until there is only one federal state in the world that has a direct democratic constitution. The communitarisation of humanity is then considered complete.

In the inner ring, the same civil participation rights, political rights and human rights apply to all citizens of a federal state. Exceptions and restrictions can be allowed within cultural protection areas as long as they remain in line with the constitution. This creates niches for minorities to create space for strictly religious, nationalistic, language or tradition-conscious citizens and other subcultures, even in the global federal state. Cultural protection areas[69] can accordingly be the size of a member state, a region of several municipalities or a city.

5.8.2.3.1 Constitutional negotiations[70]

Into the inner ring of full political integration, member states advance from the outer or middle ring by conducting constitutional negotiations and having all the peoples involved agree to the individual articles of the constitution or the

---

68 Ministry of State Organisation - 9.11 Constitutional Amendments
69 Ministry of Integration - 6.3 Cultural protection area
70 §55.5 Communitarisation of states

overall draft constitution. These constitutional negotiations must involve as many member states from all rings as possible. All member states of the International Union are involved in the voting on the constitution of the first federal state in the inner ring, even if this does not necessarily mean that they become members of the inner ring if they do not yet wish or are unable to fulfil the requirements for this. In view of a future entry into the inner ring, it is advisable to find out as early as possible which constitution the citizens of all member states would be prepared to accept. This procedure is repeated whenever a new member state joins the inner ring and the constitution is to be changed. In this way, all citizens of the International Union have the opportunity to express their opinion on the constitution of the inner ring several times and at intervals. This is to avoid the formation of several federal states in the inner ring, but not to prevent it.

The constitution in the inner ring must be approved by all citizens of the accession countries with a majority of 90%. In this voting, the population of the accession country can veto it as soon as 65% are in favour. With this veto they can demand changes to the constitution.

The population of the member states votes on whether the accession country may join. It must agree with a majority of 90%. If there is a veto, it decides whether the constitution should be amended or not. If the constitution is not to be amended, the acceding country cannot join. If the constitution is amended, the voting on the new constitution is also a vote on accession.

6 Continental policy

States that have a culturally similar population and are located in local proximity to each other on the same continent pursue a continental policy. For this purpose, they establish a Continental Union modelled on the International Union and create continental departments in all affected ministries. This strengthens the coexistence of neighbouring peoples and economic exchange and democratically avoids conflicts.

Other future goals of the Continental Union are enlargement, division of labour and communitarisation. The strategic priorities of when to align, adapt or communitarise the Continental Union are voted on with the peoples of all member states. The voting result indicates which member states are aiming for which locations in the three rings of integration.

Examples from the European Union are used below and are listed in footnotes. They should be seen as proposals for similar continental requirements or agencies.

6.1 Democratic Continental Union

The Minister of Foreign Affairs is responsible to the people for democratically involving them in governance in accordance with the constitution. This is equally true if the state is in a confederation, such as the Continental Union, or a federal state, such as the United States of the Continents. Therefore, the Minister of Foreign Affairs has a duty to the Continental Union to make the country's membership conditional on direct democratic citizen participation without chains of legitimacy. This means the direct election of politicians who are responsible for decisions of Continental Union institutions, or direct voting on individual decisions such as treaties or laws.

As a general rule, state relations with foreigners may only be diplomatic if the foreign country is not democratically governed. Since the state may only communitarise with democratically governed states in an International Union, any cooperation in the Continental Union must be democratic. The domestic people decide how much time they allow the Continental Union to democratise. In case of doubt, the foreign minister must protect his own people from undemocratic disenfranchisement and is liable for this with his deselection quorum.

6.2 Institutions of the Continental Union

The institutions of the Continental Union are different in the rings of integration. On the outer ring, there is only the Union institution which, in the course of communitarisation, takes over the functions of the Ministry of State Organisation for all member states. On the middle ring, there are the international councils for parties, ministers and deputy ministers.[71] On the inner ring, it is all the institutions described in the Ministry of State Organisation and the ministries.

6.2.1 Right to vote

On the outer ring, the right to vote for Continental Union citizens to the continental party council is made possible in all member states as long as no ministry is communitarised in the middle ring. In principle, all electoral rolls must first be digitised and shared with all member states to exclude multiple elections. Continental Union citizens with nationals of more than one member state may only exercise the right to vote in one member state.

6.2.2 Ombudsman

The Continental Ombudsman is directly elected by the citizens of all member states. He may not hold any other state office and acts independently. He is endowed with certain rights which enable him to obtain secret information from all bodies. However, secret information may not be passed on. He investigates grievances against authorities and institutions of the Continental Union on his own initiative or on the basis of a complaint. Complaints can be submitted by Continental Union citizens or residents, companies, non-governmental organisations or foundations of a member state. The Continental Ombudsman's Office is the agency of the Continental Ombudsman. It operates a liaison network of ombudsmen in all Member States. This allows complainants

---

71 Ministry of State Organisation - 8.6.3 International Council, 8.6.4.3 International Party Council

to receive assistance at all appropriate points.[72]

In the course of communitarisation, the Ombudsman becomes the Federal Moderator and the Ombudsman's Office becomes part of the Federal Moderator's Office.[73] Persons cannot fully know which agency or which body at which political level is responsible for a problem or information. Therefore, the Federal Moderator's Office can be the first point of contact, naming all the necessary offices or contacting them itself and then informing the person affected as quickly as possible.

6.3 Representation at the Continental Union

The Ministry of Foreign Affairs maintains a representation at the Continental Union, which assumes the tasks of an embassy for the International Union. It is supported in its work by the embassies and consulates in all member states of the Continental Union. The representation supports the ministries with all necessary information from the institutions of the Continental Union and gives advice to the domestic members of the Council of Ministers and the Party Council when they meet at continental level. The representation has a department for each ministry. Once all member states are part of the Continental Union unification, the representation to the Continental Union is dissolved.

The head of the representation is the representative to the Continental Union. He is the link between the ministers or heads of state and the Union institution. He prepares and follows up on meetings of domestic politicians in Continental Union institutions, especially in the International Council.

The Representation is the link between all the ministries of the member states, the Continental Union institutions and the Foreign Office. It sends staff from the relevant departments to the Council working groups that prepare the meetings of the International Council. In the course of the communitarisation of the Ministry of Foreign Affairs, staff from the Representation is seconded to the continental Foreign Office.

---

72 https://www.ombudsman.europa.eu/de/european-network-of-ombudsmen/about/de

73 Ministry of State Organisation - 4.4 Federal Moderator's Office

In order to query the interests of the ministries and to assess the interests of foreigner member states, the Continental Union Coordination Group meets. Depending on the individual case, different departments and ministries are involved in the meetings. The group consists of staff from the representation to the Continental Union and ambassadors from the affected member states, as well as staff from the Foreign Office and the heads of the Continental Department from the ministries affected.

For the exchange of information and rapid communication in crisis situations, the representation operates a communication network. This communication channel ensures an immediate exchange of information between the international council, the Continental Union institution and the representatives of all member states at the Continental Union. Through this network, information is exchanged on preliminary negotiations and follow-up for the implementation of deciders. In addition, documents for decision-making can be processed in urgent cases.

6.3.1 Legal adviser

The Foreign Office handles mediation with the ministries. In order to be able to provide the ministries with legally appropriate advice, the representation organises the legal advisors for the Foreign Office. Legal advisers must have specialist knowledge of the legal situation in the Continental Union or a Member State. Representation staff from the department for the appropriate remit, are the legal advisers for Continental Union policy, i.e. all laws that have already been unified continentally. Staff from the embassies in Continental Union member states are legal advisers for policies that have not yet been communitarised. The legal advisers also assist the representative in proceedings before continental courts.

6.3.2 Transition of the Continental Union to the middle ring

The Continental Union is gradually being transformed and democratised into the middle ring of an International Union. While candidate countries are at the outer end of the outer ring, member states of the Continental Union have already advanced further inwards.

First, in the outer ring, more and more similar laws are enacted, tasks are coordinated with each other, information is shared and authorities are networked. The national ministers and the international council are responsible for the governments in these individual cases. As soon as an authority is communitarised, the head of that authority is elected directly by all Continental Union citizens as a continental politician.

As soon as the first member states communitarise the first ministry with each other, the middle ring is considered opened. A ministry is not considered communitarised until the international minister is directly elected by all Continental Union citizens.[74] The new election of continental politicians is done by quorum.[75] Directly elected ministers can enact or revise laws together with the peoples of the member states.[76]

In the short term, a new Continental Union treaty will be drawn up for the new election and legislative processes of the middle ring. This treaty does not have to be joined by all member states of the outer ring, but only by those states that see an advantage in aspiring to the middle ring and if the majority of their population agrees. All other member states continue to work with treaties that they negotiate with each other mainly diplomatically and, if possible, democratically.

The outer and middle ring is the homeland of any number of confederations, for example, the monetary union[77] is considered a financial policy confederation, just as the Schengen area[78] is considered an economic policy confederation. It is up to the politicians and citizens of a member state to decide when and

---

74 Ministry of State Organisation - 9.9 Election of persons, 11.4.2.1 International election of persons
75 Ministry of State Organisation - 9.5.10 Deselection quorum
76 Ministry of State Organisation - 9.10 Legislation
77 https://www.consilium.europa.eu/de/council-eu/eurogroup/
78 https://ec.europa.eu/home-affairs/sites/homeaffairs/files/e-library/docs/ schengen_brochure/schengen_brochure_dr3111126_de.pdf

how quickly to pursue the path of continental integration via the International Union's three rings of integration procedures. The number of ministries and rings of integration dictate the number of intermediate goals until communitarisation is achieved. If member states are too different, they can form themselves into up to 2 ministries. In the middle ring, for example, there can be only one Ministry of Family Affairs, but two different Ministries of Education.

In the medium term, the success of less bureaucracy, uniform laws, clear responsibility and direct democratic participation by all nationals should speak for itself. This should convince all states and citizens on the continent to join the United States of the Continents.

6.3.3 Transition of the Continental Union into the inner ring

Gradually, more and more ministries are communitarised and are increasingly guided by the constitution of the inner ring. As soon as the last ministries are to be communitarised, the population of the middle ring member state and the population of the inner ring must vote on joining and jointly confirm the constitution or amend individual articles. At least two middle ring member states must jointly adopt a constitution that is approved by both peoples with a majority of at least 90% in order to open the inner ring. All member states of the Continental Union and all third countries in the continental area of expansion are involved in the constitution-making procedure[79] in order to find commonalities and differences among the continental peoples as early as possible. If the differences are nevertheless too great, up to 3 federal states can be formed, which later communitarise.

---

79 Ministry of State Organisation - 9.11 Constitutional Amendments

6.4 Shifting political contents to the policy of dynamic media democracy

The Continental Union is responsible for an increasing amount of political contents, which it describes jointly in treaties and laws and administers with joint agencies. However, the responsibility does not always lie equally with all member states, but there are different speeds, for example not all member states have the same currency or are part of an area with open borders. These states reflect the different speed of integration in the different member states and are transferred to the three rings of integration.

6.4.1 Entry and exit procedures

Before entrance into a ring of integration, the people decide whether to adopt, adapt or reject the Continental Union law in force there. The same voting can be called during membership on the repeal quorum. In the case of adoption, the Continental Department formulates the Continental Union law into identical legislative proposals and works with existing agencies, governments and courts. In the case of adaptation, attempts are made to amend contentious passages in Continental Union law in cooperation with the representation to the Continental Union with the member states.

Since it is not within the power of the Ministry of Foreign Affairs to force other states to make changes, the Ministry of Foreign Affairs negotiates the changes democratically with all the peoples involved. If no agreement is reached, the rejection comes into force. In the case of rejection, an attempt is made to declare only individual paragraphs invalid inland. If this is not possible, the exit from the respective treaty or the termination of the treaty negotiations takes place. If exit from individual treaties is not possible, exit from the inner or middle ring of the Continental Union takes place. Exit from the outer ring is only possible if a new International Union is founded or if there is a change to the International Union of another continent. In the case of an exit from the Continental

Union, the foreign minister founds another International Union on the continent and seeks like-minded states for communitarisation. Any Continental Union law with which the population still agrees applies there. All member states can join the new International Union and remain members of the Continental Union in whole or in part. In that case, the aim is for the new International Union and the Continental Union to communitarise in the middle or inner ring in order to create the unified states of the continent after all.

6.4.2 Continental Economic Union

The continental economic union is the communitarisation of the ministries of labour and economy. In the course of communitarisation, ministries of economy for Barter Economy, Planned Economy, Social Market Economy and Free Market Economy must be established to complete the middle ring economic union.

Continental economic policy focuses on the internal market. The internal market consists of the continental economic union, in whose economic area[80] no tariffs are levied and where free trade prevails. Free trade means uniform standards for production and trade of goods and services, which all member states of the economic union have set by treaty or law[81] . Member states from the outer ring can agree on the rules of the internal market through international treaties, member states from the middle ring regulate the rules of the internal market in laws. Internal markets of the outer and middle ring can merge if the treaty articles and legal texts are identical.

The Minister for Foreign Affairs, in voting with the Ministers for Economic Affairs and Labour, ensures the representation of the interests of domestic citizens in the negotiations on the rules of the internal market. To solve problems in handling the rules of the Single Market between citizens, companies and authorities, each Ministry of Foreign Affairs of the Member

---

80https://www.europarl.europa.eu/factsheets/de/sheet/169/der-europaische-wirtschaftsraum-ewr-die-schweiz-und-der-norden
81https://www.efta.int/

States operates an agency at the Ombudsman[82] . The financial aspects of the Single Market include the harmonisation of taxes, prices and fees for the same goods or services. Harmonisation follows a strategy of catching up living standards instead of redistributing wealth or lowering living standards in some Member States.

6.4.2.1 Continental Monetary Union

Continental monetary union is a communitarisation of the ministries of economics, labour and finance, which is proceeding at different speeds. While economically similar countries have a common currency, the remaining member states are not ready for it, but share a common economic and financial policy.[83]

In the course of communitarisation, the different speeds are abolished so that the continental Central Bank is subordinate to a continental Ministry of Finance. The international currency, the Free Market Economy, represents the foreign economic policy of the member states. The other currencies become continental tradable as soon as the same laws apply in all participating economic forms of the member states.

The Capital Markets Union gives continental investors the opportunity to invest capital in the member states of the Single Market. As a result, they benefit from uniform rules which they, as continental investors and Continental Union citizens, can also help to determine. In return, the national economies in the Single Market grow together and create innovative values based on the division of labour, which increase living standards and returns. Citizens of the Single Market are given direct democratic influence to help determine the requirements of the law and state measures. Citizens can change or deselect the laws and responsible politicians through quorums, committees and voting.

82https://www.bmwi.de/Redaktion/DE/Artikel/Europa/solvit-effiziente-problemloesung.html
83https://eur-lex.europa.eu/summary/chapter/economic_and_monetary_affairs.html?root_default=SUM_1_CODED=14

6.4.2.2 Economic integration

In order to achieve economic integration as quickly as possible, the fastest possible increase in the standard of living in backward member states is promoted through export controls. Export controls in the internal market can occur if relocation, energy shortages or raw material exploitation can be effectively prevented with them.

In order to generate uniform wages and prices within the internal market as quickly as possible, company locations may not be relocated to member states whose price level is 5% lower than the company's country of origin. This is to prevent the outflow of profits to the richer member state. For example, Frankfurt Airport operates an airport in Bulgaria and thus generates profits that flow to Germany instead of strengthening purchasing power in Bulgaria. In this way, the Continental Union is more like an imperial colonial power and prevents communitarisation, which is why such action is inadmissible.

In order to establish uniform living and production conditions as quickly as possible, energy and raw material policies are being unified in the internal market. Energy supply will be ensured through shared networks for electricity, gas and water, as well as through sufficient and coordinated energy production. The extraction of raw materials is coordinated between the member states in such a way that prices are the same everywhere as well as the rate of extraction. This is to prevent the exploitation of one member state to the benefit of other member states. In order to avoid the extraction of raw materials, a circular economy is pursued with as few gaps as possible. The Minister of Foreign Affairs, in voting with the Minister of Infrastructure, advocates the inclusion of the corresponding rules in the negotiations.[84]

If export controls are not sufficient to prevent damage from unemployment, the continental globalisation fund[85] will be used. It supports measures to retrain, integrate or start a business for workers in the domestic market who have

---

84 Ministry of Infrastructure - 4.3 Raw materials, 6 Networks, 9 Energy
85 https://eur-lex.europa.eu/legal-content/DE/
TXT/?uri=LEGISSUM:c10155

become unemployed due to relocation. The fund is financed through relocation fees. The fees have to be paid by companies relocating. The amount of the fees depends on the number and qualifications of the employees made redundant. The responsibility lies with the Ministry of Planned Economy under the Continental Union Social Policy.

6.4.2.3 Future economic development of the Continental Union

Free trade, which is a new form of imperialism in which wage dumping flourishes and production sites are relocated to countries with lower living standards, is prohibited. The goal is a division of labour in technology focal points so that not all countries compete globally beyond their self-sufficient basic supply, but form synergies.

Companies providing basic supplies, such as food production and retail, electricity, data and transport networks, must be owned by each member state or its citizens, as long as the relevant ministry of labour, economy or infrastructure is not communitarised. This avoids exporting profits from poorer to richer member states so as not to slow down the equalisation of living standards.

Economically, there should be better relations with neighbouring continents in the short term, rather than with remote continents. Trade and transport in particular are to be expanded. In the Continental Union, each member state has a role to play in the distribution of tasks to jointly promote innovation with the help of biotechnology.

6.4.2.4 Introduction of the economic forms

In the initial state of the Continental Union, only the Free Market Economy can participate in the Single Market as long as its minimum standards are met. For all the other three economic forms, it is first necessary to establish and unify the corresponding ministries of economy. The other three economic forms are only established in those member states that are willing to do so. By establishing the ministries along the lines of the dynamic media democracy, uniform regularisations apply to each economic form in the member states from the very beginning. For communitarisation in the middle ring, all that is then needed is the direct election of ministers for Labour, Social Market Economy, Planned Economy and Barter Economy.[86] The Free Market Economy represents the initial situation that applies in all member states. As soon as the other three economic forms are established, all laws in the Free Market Economy that are already covered by the other three economic forms can be dismantled. Different tax rates in different Member States of the same economic form are prohibited. Uniformly different tax rates between the different economic forms are allowed. As soon as the same standards apply in an economic form, goods and services may be traded without restriction and company locations may be relocated.[87] As long as the laws of all economic forms are the same, free movement between all four economic forms is possible.

6.4.2.4.1 Free Market Economy

Companies in the Free Market Economy are only required to comply with existing Continental Union law and the requirements of their ministry. Free Market Economy labour unions are given the rights to organise continental industrial action and to strike.[88] There is no formation phase of ministries of Free Market Economy because all current ministries of economy are considered ministries of Free Market Economy. Only when the other economic forms have been established will the Ministry of Free Market Economy hand over its identically worded responsibilities to the new ministries of economy.

---

86 Ministry of Labour - 8 Theory of Hybrid Economic Systems
87 Ministry of Labour - 22.1 Introduction of economic forms
88 Ministry of Free Market Economy - 7.3 Trade Unions

6.4.2.4.2 Social Market Economy

Member states must introduce compulsory insurance and a national currency. Companies wishing to join the Social Market Economy must adhere to appropriate requirements, which are verified and certified by the Company Auditing Agency. Once a continental Ministry of Labour is established, standards can be uniformly audited and certified continent-wide by the Company Auditing Agency. The Social Market Economies of the member states can trade capital assets, goods and services on a continental basis and introduce a currency for this purpose. The currency is managed by a single Note-issuing Bank, which is also part of the continental Central Bank. As soon as all national inequalities in the laws of the Social Market Economy are dismantled and the compulsory insurance funds are communitarised, the currency is switched from the national currency to the continental currency. The continental currency is the currency of the Social Market Economy in the middle ring. As soon as member states communitarise in the inner ring, the continental currency becomes the national currency of the continent. The Free Market Economy continues to trade in its international currency. The Free Market Economy's currency is the only currency that can be traded internationally. The continental currency remains the currency of the Social Market Economy, which may only be traded within the member states of communitarised ministries for the Social Market Economy. The process is repeated as soon as the unified continental states communitarise with another continental union.

6.4.2.4.3 Planned Economy[89]

Planned Economy companies are entitled to trade with Member States of the Single Market if demand is met in all Social Villages. Experimental Enterprises, Innovation Enterprises and People's Innovation Companies[90] are fully entitled to trade with other economic forms and the Member

---

89 §225.4 Foreign economic policy
90 Ministry of Innovation - 10 People's Innovation Company

States of the internal market at any time. Restrictions can only be set by Social Villagers by quorum and voting.

To implement the Planned Economy, Member States must establish and operate Social Villages where volunteers, those on social assistance and the unemployed can live.[91] Persons from other Continental Union member states can only benefit from Planned Economy social welfare when their member state also provides social welfare to the same extent or the resources of the continental funds are sufficient. More details are described in the Continental Union Social Policy.

The Planned Economy can be established at any time by Member States in small or large, several or few Social Villages. All state entrepreneurs or companies under public law are incorporated into the Planned Economy. Member States' Planned Economy may trade with each other without restriction as long as they abide by the same laws.

6.4.2.4.4 Barter Economy[92]

Barter Economy companies are not allowed to sell their goods abroad, but only inland in the capital cities of the Barter Economy Zones[93] . However, Barter Economy companies are entitled to exchange their goods with other Barter Economy Zones, even if the Barter Economy Zone is located in a Member State of the Internal Market.

The Barter Economy can be established at any time by Member States in many or few, small or large, preferably rural forest areas of Member States. The condition of sustainable management without the use of non-naturally degradable substances remains. Continental nationals are given freedom of movement to establish themselves in all Barter Economy Zones[94] on the continent once the ministries for Barter Economy in their member states are communitarised in the middle ring and have identified similar sized areas as Barter Economy Zones.

91 Ministry of Planned Economy - 21.8 Mobilisation
92 §225.3 Foreign economic policy
93 Ministry of Barter Economy - 6 Barter Economy Zone
94 Ministry of Barter Economy - 7 Administration of the Barter Economy Zones

6.4.3 Continental Union internal market

The Continental Single Market is a single continental market for goods, services, persons and capital. It exists to create greater equality of rights for companies and consumers.[95]

In the course of communitarisation, freedom of movement requires that there be a uniform standard of living in the internal market so that there is no exploitation of poorer states by richer states, companies or citizens. In this respect, the Continental Union internal market must guarantee to avoid a redistribution and lowering of living standards.

The reforms include tariffs on goods, services and financial products that can only be offered more cheaply because standards, taxes, wages or property prices are lower in the other member state. In these cases, Customs are allowed in order to avoid a poverty race.

6.4.3.1 Country-of-destination principle

In the Single Market, the country-of-destination principle is applied without exception. Under the country of origin principle, the rules of the country of origin apply to goods, services, financial transactions and persons. Under the country-of-destination principle, the rules of the country where the goods are used or the service is provided, the financial transaction arrives, the business location is opened, persons move there or sign an employment contract apply. The country-of-destination principle is extended in federal systems to the municipalities, where different rules may apply than in the nation.[96] Only when uniform laws in all member states guarantee equal regularisation in the country-of-origin and the country-of-destination does full freedom of movement apply.[97]

The communitarisation of the ministries of labour, economy, finance, education and integration in the middle ring completes the single market. In the outer ring, the country-

95https://eur-lex.europa.eu/summary/chapter/internal_market.
html?root_default=SUM_1_CODED=24
96Ministry of State Organisation - 11.5 Municipal policy
97Ministry of State Organisation - 11.4 Global policy

of-destination principle applies, which is losing importance due to increasing regularisation.

The value added tax of the Country-of-destination applies at the time of sale. Consumers pay it when shopping with a digital payment method or when withdrawing money before buying in cash.

6.4.3.2 Goods

The internal market for goods is characterised by the free movement of safe and uniformly tested products. To ensure that goods are recognised in all member states, they issue harmonised regulations for safe and accessible products as well as for measuring instruments, measuring and testing methods. Continental Conformity marking exists so that companies can have their products tested and marked uniformly.[98] Testing and approval is carried out in So-called accreditation bodies in the member states, which are standardised by the Continental Cooperation for Accreditation[99] . If obstacles to trade occur, there is a uniform intervention mechanism.[100]

In the course of communitarisation, the safest requirements are adopted and guaranteed by the test seals.[101] Continental norms are aligned with current Company Auditing Agency standards in voting with the Ministry of Labour. Import restrictions will apply to goods that do not meet the safety standards.[102] In the course of communitarisation, standards for the production of goods are also aligned.

If taxes, wages or real estate prices are lower in the Country-of-origin than in the Country-of-destination, the difference is levied as a Customs to exclude competitive disadvantages in the Country-of-origin or exploitation in the Country-of-

---

98https://eur-lex.europa.eu/legal-content/DE/
TXT/?uri=legissum%3Al33248 https://eur-lex.europa.eu/legal-content/
DE/TXT/?uri=legissum%3Al10141
99https://european-accreditation.org/
100https://eur-lex.europa.eu/legal-content/DE/
TXT/?uri=legissum%3Al11042
101Ministry of Labour - 20.7.4.2 Seal of Approval, 17.7.4 Seal of Quality
102Ministry of Health - 6.4 Product Safety

origin. Further import restrictions and tariffs can be set by the ministries of economy to protect their economic form. For all other goods, there is a customs union. Within the Single Market there are then no Customs and all goods bought or sold outside the Single Market are subject to uniform tariffs. Customs are levied on deliveries of goods from or to developing countries to compensate for or prevent damage in the developing countries.[103]

6.4.3.3 Services

Services in the internal market can still be provided by companies of one Member State in any other Member State, for example by craftspersons. Similarly, citizens of any Member State can also use services in any other Member State, as tourists do, for example. Service providers pay taxes in the Member State where they have registered their company. If the taxes in the Country-of-origin and Country-of-destination are different, Customs are levied to compensate for the differences. To clear customs, service providers from continental foreign countries must open an online account with the People's Bank. There, their earnings are deposited, Customs are deducted and the remaining amount is transferred to the account in the country of origin.

In order to ensure sufficient qualification for a service, the educational qualifications of all member states are voted on and recognised. If there is no sufficient qualification for the Country-of-destination, the service may not be provided. Labour and environmental protection standards[104] must be met in all economic forms. The Ministry of Labour sets the limits for the freedom to provide services until all labour ministries are communitarised. This applies in particular to social security, employment exchange, training, standards and freedom of movement on the internal market.[105] This is to prevent social dumping. To avoid wage dumping, all labour

103 Ministry of Labour - 10.3 Foreign Trade Regulations
104 Ministry of Labour - 14.2 Occupational safety and health, 14.3 Environmental protection
105 Ministry of Labour - 11 Labour Policy, 12 Employment Office, 16 Employee Protection

unions in the member states are encouraged to negotiate continental collective labour agreements. Depending on the economic form, uniform collective agreements on wages and working conditions are obligatory in order to be allowed to participate in the continental single market.[106]

6.4.3.4 Persons

In the Single Market, citizens are free to choose their place of residence, employment and training. However, citizens from other Member States must comply with the requirements of the Country-of-destination when they take up employment or become employers. In order to bring the country-of-origin and the Country-of-destination together, the ministries of labour and economy communitarise their enterprise policies.[107] As soon as the member states are communitarised in the inner ring, nationals of the member states may buy land in all new parts of the country. Until then, the principle applies that only nationals may own the national territory.[108]

In order to establish borderless freedom of movement for persons in the internal market, border controls on persons are abolished in the border area of the Continental Union and only maintained at the external borders of the Continental Union. This communitarisation is ensured by the ministries of security and justice.

6.4.3.4.1 Social security

Social security schemes cover sickness, accidents at work, parenthood, family benefits, pensions and unemployment. They are coordinated continentally so that entitlements are also claimed in another member state and granted across borders. As part of the communitarisation, the Ministries of Labour offer Citizens' Insurance[109] so that nationals of other Member

---

106 Ministry of Labour - 9 Principles of hybrid economic systems, 10 Freedom of movement between economic forms
107 Ministries of Labour and Economic Affairs - Enterprise policy
108 Ministry of Labour - 19.6 Land market
109 Ministry of Labour - 10.2.4 Citizens' Insurance

States can transfer their insurance contributions without loss, provided their insurance company has an agreement with Citizens' Insurance. Through the communitarisation of the Ministries of Health, Labour and Economy, health, social and pension insurance schemes are unified.[110] All citizens of the Single Market will be able to transfer their private pensions without loss when moving between two Member States and using Citizens' Insurance.

6.4.3.4.2 Guest workers from Member States and third countries

For third-country workers, treaties are negotiated and voted on by the affected peoples on how multinational companies can send their third-country workers to the Continental Union.[111] With communitarisation, the free movement of persons in the internal market applies to all nationals of the member states, as long as this complies with the requirements of the Ministry of Integration[112] . Immigration rights and obligations provide for simpler procedures for Continental Union citizens. The quota of foreigners sets a maximum of 20% Continental Union citizens in the total domestic population. This limit can be adjusted or abolished in the course of the communitarisation of the Ministry of Integration after a voting in all member states.

6.4.3.4.3 Authorities for the free movement of persons

The Law Directory is used for information on rights, the Company Auditing Agency for free advice and problem solving, the Continental Employment Office for unification, the Labour Directory for continental search and advertisement of jobs, and the Education Directory for proof

---

110 Ministry of Health - 5.12 Health Insurance, Ministry of Planned Economy - 17.1 Social welfare, Ministry of Labour - 21 Pension
111 https://eur-lex.europa.eu/summary/chapter/2402.html
112 Ministry of Integration - 7.1 Rights and obligations, 9.2 Withdrawal of domestic citizenship, 7.4 Quota of foreigners

of qualifications.[113]

6.4.3.4.4 Border area

The border area of the Continental Union is an area on the continent where no border controls are carried out. In the common information system[114], all security agencies of the Member States share their data on the tracing of persons and objects. The Continental Police organises cooperation between the security agencies of the Member States in cross-border searches and investigations. The Continental Public Prosecutor's Office coordinates cooperation between the judicial authorities of the Member States. The communitarisation is described in detail in the Continental Union Security Policy and the Continental Union Justice Policy.

6.4.3.5 Capital

Payment transactions within the Single Market are carried out in the Continental Payments Area. This means that all persons and companies can send money without hindrance. As long as the Ministries of Finance are not communitarised in the middle ring, the payment regulations of the Country-of-destination apply. All banks in the member states are connected via the international telecommunications network for banks (SWIFTNet)[115]. Each financial institution is assigned an account number at the Central Bank, the So-called Business Identifier Code (BIC)[116]. The organisation for worldwide financial telecommunications between banks (SWIFT)[117] will be restricted to banks in the Single Market in

---

113 Ministry of Justice - 4.7 Law Directory, Ministry of Labor - 20
Company Auditing Agency, 12 Employment Office, 13 Labour
Directory, Ministry of Education - 5.9 Education Directory
114 https://edps.europa.eu/data-protection/european-it-systems/
schengen-information-system_de
115 https://www.swift.com/our-solutions/interfaces-and-integration/
swiftnet-link
116 https://www.swift.com/standards/data-standards/bic-business-
identifier-code
117 https://www.swift.com/

the course of communitarisation in the Capital Markets Union and administered by the Central Bank. This is to guarantee the security and legality of all financial transactions in the Single Market. Financial transactions into the Single Market or out of the Continental Payments Area will be routed via the Central Bank to the international telecommunications network for banks. This is to prevent tax evasion and money laundering. Further requirements, measures and authorities for the freedom of movement for chapters are described in the Continental Union Capital Markets Union and Continental Union Monetary Union.

The movement of capital within the internal market is unrestricted as long as it does not increase or decrease prices in a member state. The movement of capital between the internal market and abroad is restricted because this is intended to prevent foreign influence on the internal market. The amount of money and securities flowing out of the internal market abroad can be restricted in quantity, as can the amount of money invested in the internal market. Customs, equivalent to business tax, is levied on income flowing out of the internal market to foreign countries, So-called third countries.

6.4.4 Continental Union Investment Policy

Part of the continental economic policy is investment. In the course of communitarisation, the national state banks and development banks, including their fund management, become part of the newly founded continental People's Bank. Foreign direct investments are only possible there indirectly via the Continental Fund. Foreign direct investments are otherwise only possible in the Free Market Economy and Social Market Economy.

6.4.4.1 Continental People's Bank

With the communitarisation of the Ministry of Finance, a state bank for the internal market is established. This state bank is called the Continental People's Bank. When it is founded, all the peoples of the member states directly elect the head of the Continental People's Bank. The Continental People's Bank then also operates a Continental People's Stock Exchange and Ideas Stock Exchange.[118] The auditing of companies and states is done by the Company Auditing Agency once the Ministry of Labour is communitarised. Therefore, the People's Stock Exchange and Ideas Stock Exchange may not be applied in the domestic market until the Company Auditing Agency and the CRA have become operational in all member states. Foreign investors and companies are not allowed to participate in the People's Stock Exchange and Ideas Stock Exchange.

All nationals of Member States in the Single Market can trade People's Shares and People's Bonds on the People's Stock Exchange. Member States can issue government bonds and also real estate bonds once the Ministry of Infrastructure is communitarised. Companies of all sizes can issue People's Shares or launch People's Bonds. On the Ideas Stock Exchange, inventors or entrepreneurs from Member States can issue Innovation Bonds or issue Innovation Shares, Licensing Shares or Product Shares. Nationals of Member States can invest in them. The Continental People's Bank operates pension accounts for retirement savings, which can be invested in funds, such as the People's Fund and the Real Estate Fund. For foreigners, there are the Continental Funds, which are equivalent to the Domestic Funds but extended to the Member States of the Single Market.[119]

In this way, the Ministry of Finance reduces the risk for investors in the Capital Markets Union so that the financing of small and medium-sized companies, as well as retirement provisions, is as secure as possible.[120] The investment department of the continental People's Bank is responsible for fund management and state investments in order to invest saved state assets as profitably and sustainably as possible.[121] In the course of the communitarisation of the Ministry of Innovation, the Funds for Innovation, People's Innovation Company and Research

118 Ministry of Finance - 11.8 People's Stock Exchange, 11.9 Ideas Stock Exchange
119 Ministry of Finance - 11.11 Funds
120 Ministry of Finance - 11.10 Risk
121 Ministry of Finance - 11.12 Investment Department

Projects will also become part of the Ideas Stock Exchange.[122]

6.4.5 Continental Union Capital Markets Union

The Capital Markets Union is intended to enable companies to obtain money on the continental capital market and not only from banks. In the course of communitarisation, the ministries of finance, labour and economics form a Capital Markets Union to regularise capital movements in the Single Market. In the Capital Markets Union, all laws are harmonised. This includes securities law for shares and bonds, rules for joint-stock companies, business taxes for investors, in short the rules for the finance economy of the ministries of labour and economics.[123]

In the course of the communitarisation of the Ministry of Labour, the handling of an insolvency of companies is uniformly regulated in the internal market. The same applies to the laws of the finance economy, which apply to all economic forms. This includes money games, stock exchange maturity, stock exchange trading and joint-stock companies.[124] Communitarisation also means that legal rules on environmental and occupational safety and health are adopted. Capital can thus no longer be invested in environmentally harmful, belligerent or exploitative companies.[125]

6.4.5.1 Continental Financial Supervisory Authority

Continental authorities supervise insurance companies, banks and securities markets in the Continental Union. In the course of communitarisation, the continental financial supervisory authorities are merged and run by a directly elected politician. The authorities of the finance economy, responsible for all

---

122 Ministry of Innovation - 5.3.1 Research Cost Fund, 9.11.1.1 Innovation Fund, 10.3.5 People's Innovation Company Fund
123 Ministries of Labour and Economic Affairs - Finance economy
124 Ministry of Labour - 14.9 Insolvency, 18 Finance economy
125 Ministry of Labour - 14.3 Environmental protection, 14.2 Occupational safety and health, 10.3 Foreign trade regulations

economic forms, consist of the Financial Supervisory Authority for banks, stock exchanges and insurance companies as well as the rating agency.[126] Uniform rules are drawn up and adopted for the Financial Supervisory Authority.[127] Their compliance is checked by audit services.[128] A central component is the Company Auditing Agency, which ensures compliance with fair competition standards through its audits and provides investors with reliable government and company data through its audit results.[129] The Note-issuing Banks undertake the money supply and settlement of the banks in their economic form. The Central Bank is not an agency of the finance economy, but an agency for the management of the Note-issuing Banks and the economy as a whole.[130]

6.4.6 Continental Union Monetary Union

The continental monetary union is characterised by the fact that all its member states issue a common international currency in which they trade together. Like any currency, its value is linked to the economy in which it is generated through wages and prices. Its value is measured by how many goods and services are implemented through it. Once the Ministries of Finance are communitarised, the value of the currency increases by the state's foreign reserves.

In the monetary union, all member states pursue a uniform exchange rate and currency policy as soon as the common agreements are fulfilled and adhered to. This regulates the currency area, the currency, the responsible institutions of the monetary union, exchange rate issues and protection against money counterfeiting.[131]

In the course of communitarisation, the Continental Central Bank administers the international currency of the Free Market Economy in the outer ring until the Ministries of

126 Ministry of Labour - 14.9 Insolvency, 18 Finance economy
127 Ministry of Labour - 18.3 Financial Supervisory Authority
128 Ministries of media, security, justice, finance, labour, state organisation - 2.1.2.1 Audit services
129 Ministry of Labor - 20 Company Auditing Agency
130 Ministry of Finance - 10.4 Note-issuing Banks, 10 Central Bank
131 https://eur-lex.europa.eu/summary/chapter/1405.html

Finance are communitarised.

The member states in the currency area jointly form a government for the regularisation, administration and stabilisation of the continental currency. The finance ministers and their deputies form an international council for currency policy.[132]

6.4.6.1 Conditions for communitarisation of a currency

All member states of the monetary union must have at least one Free Market Economy. If they have other economic forms, these have their own currency. Once ministries of finance and the Barter Economy, Planned Economy or Social Market Economy are communitarised, these member states can each have a common currency for each economic form.

In the course of communitarisation, the admission criteria are adjusted to ensure the monetary stability of the continental currency. The requirements specify how high the debts of a ministry for Free Market Economy may be, what the minimum Gross Domestic Product in the Free Market Economy must be or how much it may fluctuate. In voting, the peoples of all member states can enter the values as numerals or reject the monetary union. The voting result is the median of all values. As soon as a member state can no longer meet the admission criteria, the withdrawal procedure is initiated. The affected member state must then leave the monetary union and re-introduce its own currency, which it can devalue and revalue accordingly. As soon as it meets the criteria again, it can re-enter. If many countries are in a similar situation, they can launch another international currency.

The additional currency has lower admission criteria, but also makes it easier for poorer countries in the International Union to trade together in order to raise their standard of living more quickly and to meet the admission criteria of the stronger continental currency. The additional currency thus becomes the currency of the outer and at most the middle ring. It will have at least one Note-issuing Bank and, if necessary, a separate Continental Ministry of Finance for member states

132Ministry of State Organisation – 8.6.3 International Council

with weaker economies, as well as an International Council of Finance Ministers for all its member states. In the medium term, the strong continental currency is to become the sole currency in the inner ring, in which there is a uniform standard of living with similar Gross Domestic Product in all parts of the country.

6.4.6.2 Continental Central Bank

The continental agency of the monetary union is the Continental Central Bank. In the course of communitarisation, it becomes the Central Bank of all Note-issuing Banks for the Free Market Economy in the Member States of the Monetary Union. It regularly prepares country analyses of all member states of the monetary union for the international council of finance ministers. In order to cope with financial crises, it can apply measures in the event of inflation or deflation.[133] The purchase programme of securities on the international financial market is limited to the purchase of bonds of continental states and companies.

As long as the Ministry of Finance is not communitarised, it is not a state bank but a continental Note-issuing Bank of the Ministries of Outer and Middle Ring Free Market Economy. The responsibilities of a Central Bank are regulated by the Ministry of Finance.[134] As long as the head of the Continental Central Bank is not directly elected by the peoples of the member states, the foreign minister must be able to influence the decisions of the head of the Continental Central Bank in the interests of the people. This influence is exercised in cooperation with the Minister of Finance within the framework of the responsibilities of a Central Bank and its tools.[135] If this is not possible, the foreign minister is liable with his deselection quorum or can withdraw from the monetary union.

---

133 Ministry of Finance - 10.8 Measures in the event of inflation or deflation
134 Ministry of Finance - 10 Central Bank
135 Ministry of Finance - 10.3 Tools of the Central Bank

6.4.6.3 Currency stabiliser

A fund is established to stabilise the continental currency. The money currently issued by the Continental Central Bank is to be deposited in this fund in cash and giro money. The fund is composed of 80% commodities and 20% foreign currencies. Each member of the monetary union must pay into this fund at the beginning until the Gross Domestic Product of a year has been paid in. If a country has gold reserves, it can use this gold as a direct deposit and settle it at the current gold price. The shares that each individual country must pay in are measured by the total turnover in the continental currency in one year in the entire currency area, divided by the total turnover of the participating country in the same year. The countries of the monetary union all have a different Gross Domestic Product, which varies annually among the different participants. To harmonise these fluctuations, the fund is designed to be dynamic.

6.4.6.3.1 Receipts and disbursements from the fund

Each member state of the monetary union must show on its fund deposit with the Continental Central Bank the account balance equal to the Gross Domestic Product of the previous year. If the Gross Domestic Product of a monetary union member has grown, it must pay in the amount by which it has grown. If the Gross Domestic Product of a currency union member has shrunk, it is paid the amount by which it has shrunk. This creates a counter-cyclical investment opportunity.

6.4.6.3.2 Fund management

With the money paid in by the member states, the fund management buys non-perishable commodities that are scarce on the continent, have to be imported and whose value increases. If sufficient capacity is built up on the continent, the scarce commodities are sold as long as the new capacities do not yet cause prices to fall. The same applies to imported goods. Currencies are bought that are at a low level and are expected to rise. The fund management receives information from the embassies about the state of the country and about the effects of planned policy decisions through communitarisation or development aid with the country issuing the currency in question.

The currencies of large economic areas such as China, Europe, Russia, India or the USA are bought and sold in proportion to their strong performance. If the trend is downwards, they are sold and if the trend is upwards, they are bought.

6.4.7 Continental Union Social Policy

The social benefits of the member states are increasingly paid into a social fund which is used to build a Planned Economy and to house needy Continental Union citizens.[136]

The Ministry of Planned Economy operates a continental social policy[137] , through which the unemployed, disabled and pensioners from other member states can live in the Planned Economy, provided they either have appropriate insurance or if the member states have paid enough into the social fund. The Ministry of Planned Economy can make it possible for a corresponding number of Continental Union citizens to stay in the Planned Economy through compensation payments from the Social Fund, as long as the Social Villagers do not decide against it in a voting. As soon as Barter Economy and Planned Economy zones have also been established in other member states and corresponding ministries have been set up, nationals of other member states can also live there.

The Ministries of Labour, Social Market Economy, Planned Economy and Foreigners, in cooperation with the continental Employment Office, jointly ensure the coordination of social legal systems. The Ministry of Labour ensures that guest workers from Continental Union member states can easily take their social security contributions for unemployment, pension and health with them when moving between states, without

---

136Ministry of Planned Economy - 6.1.2 necessarily moving in, 18.1.3 health centre, 18.1.6 house for disabled people, 18.1.7 children's house
137Ministry of Planned Economy - 15.1 Continental Social Policy

having to give up benefit entitlements.[138] This means that all member states have standardised their health, pension and unemployment insurance, or have concluded an agreement with Citizens' Insurance. Every citizen receives an account for their social insurances, into which contributions are paid and from which costs for social benefits are covered. Only when the accounts of all health, pension and unemployment insurances of all member states have been communitarised will there no longer be any restrictions on social insurance and the citizens of the member states will have the same rights to social welfare everywhere.[139]

The Ministry of Social Market Economy provides insurance offers with adjusted premium rates for members of other economic forms and foreigners.[140]

6.4.8 Continental Union Labour Policy

Continental labour policy regulates mobility and employment in the Continental Union, health and safety at work, labour law, protection against discrimination and agrees on a continental employment strategy.[141]

In continental collective labour agreements, the So-called social partners, consisting of representatives of employers and employees, negotiate continental agreements. Continental collective bargaining takes place in many different sectors and adapts to the Continental Union law applicable there. Employees are guaranteed information, consultation or participation. Employees can establish continental works councils and thereby have a say.

In the course of communitarisation, democratic collective bargaining is established.[142] For this purpose, the existing trade unions of the member states are mandated to unite

---

138 Ministry of Labour - 16.11 Guest work, 10.2.4 Citizens' Insurance
139 Ministry of Planned Economy - 17.1 Social welfare
140 Ministry of Social Market Economy - 10.2 Insolvency insurance, 12.3.1 Buildings insurance, 12.3.2 Buildings liability insurance, 12.3.3 Household contents insurance, 17.5 Compulsory insurances
141 https://eur-lex.europa.eu/summary/chapter/employment_and_ social_policy.html?root_default=SUM_1_CODED=17
142 Ministry of Labour - 16.8 Democratic collective bargaining

and publicly negotiate as continental labour unions with continental employers' associations in their sector a continental labour law and minimum wages for all sectors. All members of the labour unions and employers' associations vote on the outcome of the negotiations. In the event that negotiations fail, continental industrial action is permitted.[143] Only when the ministries for Social Market Economy and Planned Economy are communitarised can industrial action be stopped there.

Communitarisation combines and unifies the laws on labour policy and employee protection with the requirements on continental labour policy.[144]

Within the framework of the continental communitarisation of the Ministry of Labour, all member states must jointly create a sufficient capacity of educational places, Social Villages and jobs for all their inhabitants. Only when these capacities have been established nationwide can the Minister of Labour be directly elected and thus the Ministry of Labour communitarised.

6.4.8.1 Labour market

The continental labour market is represented by the Employment Offices of the member states and the Labour Directory.[145] In the course of communitarisation, a continental Employment Office is established and the Labour Directory is available throughout the continent. All member states pay seed capital for Experimental Enterprises and Innovation Enterprises into their funds until they become self-financing and the seed capital can be gradually withdrawn again.[146] Citizens from Continental Union member states can participate fully in the employment exchange of the Ministry of Labour, as long as the goal of full employment is not jeopardised.[147] The Ministry of Labour is responsible for measuring full

---

143 Ministry of Labour - 16.7 Industrial action
144 Ministry of Labour - 11 Labour policy, 16 Employee protection
145 Ministry of Labour - 12 Employment Office, 13 Labour Directory
146 Ministry of Planned Economy - 10.8.2 Start-up Fund, 10.6.6 Innovation Fund
147 Ministry of Labour - 12 Employment Office, 13 Labour Directory

employment and can introduce restrictions on foreigners if the labour market reaches capacity. The Company Auditing Agency measures the labour utilisation of the companies and the Labour Directory records the number and rate of vacancies and the number of job seekers. Only when the Ministries of Labour and Planned Economy are communitarised and full employment prevails throughout the continent will national or regional restrictions on foreigners from Continental Union member states become inadmissible.

6.4.8.2 Occupational safety and health

Continental occupational safety and health includes common rules for occupational safety and health to protect workers and the environment.[148] Successful policies are shared and shortcomings are addressed. The auditors of the Company Auditing Agency for Health, Technology and Innovation are responsible for this.[149]

6.4.8.3 Competition

Continental competition policy is geared towards competition for the most innovative product and a circular economy of economic forms. In the course of communitarisation, state aid is reduced. In the budget of the Continental Union, aid, also called subsidies, may only be used if it can achieve a redistribution to equalise the standard of living within the Continental Union. After that, they must also be dismantled. Exceptions in antitrust law are only allowed for innovations and Non-profit companies.[150] In the different economic forms, competition can be interfered with to varying degrees. The economic forms are in free competition with each other because workers, customers and investors can decide which

---

148 Ministry of Labour - 14.2 Occupational safety and health, 14.3 Environmental protection
149 Ministry of Labour - 20.7.2 Health auditor, 20.7.5 Innovation auditor, 20.7.4 Technical auditor, 20.9 Success Model Directory
150 Ministry of Innovation - 9.10 Cartels for Innovation, Ministry of Social Market Economy - 11.2.1 Cartels

economic form they support through their involvement. The Antitrust Agency, in cooperation with the Company Auditing Agency, is responsible for investigations, defining markets and procedures for assessing fines, approving mergers and authorising and breaking up cartels.[151]

6.4.8.4 Company

In order to unify enterprise policy, the different requirements and measures in all member states are adopted, adapted or discarded in the enterprise policy of the ministries of labour and economy.[152] In the course of communitarisation, the Law Directory will be linked to the Labour Directory to provide entrepreneurs with an overview of all rights and obligations as soon as they are established.[153] Citizens will then be able to set up continental companies, which will be treated and taxed according to the same company law in all member states.

6.4.8.4.1 Cooperation between states and companies

For continental cooperation between member states and companies, the requirements for state enterprises are standardised.[154] Cooperation between state enterprises, ministries and private companies is subject to approval. Approval is granted by the Minister of Labour at the national level, the deputy Minister of Labour at the municipal level and the Ministers of Labour of the outer ring member states at the international level. A prerequisite is that state orders are put out to public tender so that companies can apply for them. The treaties, including the cost of the orders, can be accepted or rejected by the population in the budget vote before they are signed. The publication requirement enables citizen

---

151 Ministry of Labour - 9 Principles of hybrid economic systems, 10 Free movement between economic forms, 15 Antitrust Agency, 20.7.5.6 Approval of relaxations of antitrust laws, 20.7.6.9 Compliance with antitrust laws.
152 Ministries of Labour and Economic Affairs - Enterprise policy
153 Ministry of Justice - 4.7 Law Directory, Ministry of Labour - 13 Labour Directory
154 Ministry of Labour - 4 State enterprises

intervention through a veto quorum or the cancellation of funding through majority rejection of the costs in the budget vote.[155]

6.4.8.4.2 Intellectual property

To protect intellectual property, the requirements on industrial property rights and the Patent Office are standardised. Intellectual property can be registered and marketed in the Ideas Directory.[156] To facilitate world trade with the internal market, agreements are concluded with the World Trade Organization (WTO)[157] and treaties with the World Intellectual Property Organization (WIPO) .[158]

6.4.8.5 Consumer protection

Continental consumer protection policy focuses on strengthening consumer skills and confidence.[159] It unifies consumer rights. Consumers can call consumer centres to settle disputes out of court. Or they can join together in class actions to enforce their consumer rights in court. Consumer protection law prevents unfair contract terms, guarantees rights for travellers, regulates obligations for financial services and prevents unfair business activities and unfair pricing.[160]
In the course of communitarisation, consumer protection policy is structured uniformly and effective consumer protection regulations from the member states are adopted. Consumers can make reports in the Consumer Directory, which will be checked and, if necessary, published.

---

155 Ministry of Labour - 4.5 Publication requirement, Ministry of State Organisation - 9.5.14 Veto quorum, Ministry of Finance - 9.5 Budget vote
156 Ministry of Innovation - 7.2 Industrial property rights, 8 Ideas Directory
157 https://www.wto.org/
158 https://www.wipo.int/portal/en/index.html
159 Ministry of Labour - 17 Consumer protection
160 https://eur-lex.europa.eu/summary/chapter/0904.html

6.4.9 Continental Union agricultural policy

The continental agricultural policy pursues the goals of increasing agricultural productivity, protecting consumers and the environment, and ensuring that consumers are adequately supported at reasonable prices. Common requirements on agricultural products, genetically modified organisms, pesticides and fertilisers prevent production advantages in individual member states at the expense of the environment or consumers.

In the course of communitarisation, member states' funding for agriculture is used to convert the farm to permaculture and indoor agribusiness.[161] Arable land is cultivated with permaculture and farm buildings are used for indoor agribusiness.[162] The member states combine their efforts in developing new robotics for harvesting, care and breeding. They share seeds, cultivation and breeding plans with each other. After the changeover, all direct payments to farmers will cease and funding will be reduced.

6.4.9.1 Fishing

Continental fisheries policy concerns fishing vessels, working conditions on vessels, fishing methods, fish stocks, fish farming and environmental protection. In part, international agreements already exist in this regard.[163] In the course of communitarisation, fishing is replaced by fish farming in aquacultures. Remaining fish species that cannot be farmed may only be caught with biodegradable longlines. This avoids by-catches and ghost nets. Endangered species may temporarily not be caught at all until their population has recovered. Restoration measures in inland waters enable increasing yields inland.[164] The Company Auditing Agency controls compliance with the requirements and works with

---

161 Ministry of Labour - 19.8.7.1 Conversion of agricultural land, 19.8.8.1 Agri-factories
162 Ministry of Labour - 19 Agriculture
163 https://eur-lex.europa.eu/summary/chapter/0206.html?locale=de
164 Ministry of Labour - 19.10 Fisheries policy

Customs to carry out unannounced inspections at sea.[165]

6.4.10 Continental Union Budget Policy

Continental budgetary policy differs in the different rings of integration. In the course of the communitarisation of the Ministries of Finance, the Continental Union has to provide for its own revenues in the outer ring and is only given responsibility for state revenues in the middle ring. In the outer ring, the Continental Union takes over services for its member states, which it executes on behalf of the ministries. Therefore, the ministries include the cost centres in their annual financial plans and advertise them to the population for approval in the budget vote. The controls are carried out by the audit services[166] and the audits are carried out by the Audit Court.[167]

6.4.10.1 Revenues

In the course of communitarisation, revenues are determined in the outer ring. The Minister of Foreign Affairs must negotiate with the people what forms of state revenues[168] the Continental Union may collect.

Tariffs set uniformly across the continent flow to the Continental Union as own resources. Customs duties that member states set themselves over and above this are reserved for them. 1% of the value added taxes of all member states flow to the Continental Union. Value added taxes apply equally in all economic forms, thus preventing the excessive burdening of one economic form. Revenues that benefit the Free Market Economy may only come from the Ministry of Free Market Economy, which spends part of its business taxes on it.

In future, the Continental Union will generate its own

---

165 Ministry of Labour - 20.8 Audit, Ministry of Security - 8 Tariffs
166 Ministries of media, security, justice, finance, labour, state organisation - 2.1.2.1 Audit services
167 Ministry of Finance - 8 State revenues, 9 State expenditure, 9.7 Accounting office
168 Ministry of Finance - 8 State revenues

income through its subsidies. Subsidies must be repaid with 10% interest as soon as profits are generated. 5% of the profits generated by the funding is used annually for repayment until 110% of the funding has been reimbursed. The period is flexible and not bound to any deadline. If additional funds are to flow, the people determine in the budget vote[169] how high the net payments to the Continental Union should be.

6.4.10.2 Expenditure

The Continental Union Audit Court monitors the expenditure of the Continental Union. Expenditure is administered by the Ministries of Finance and determined by the citizens. Expenditure in the outer ring is determined by the budget votes in the member states. Each ministry that uses services of the Continental Union adds these cost centres to its financial plan. The Ministry of Foreign Affairs assumes all costs of the Continental Union that cannot be allocated to individual ministries. Only in the middle ring communitarisation does a continental budget vote take place for the communitarised ministries.[170]

6.4.10.3 Communitarisation of budgetary policy

The Continental Union's revenues and expenditures differ according to their position in the rings of integration. In the outermost ring, the member states order joint projects of individual ministries of all member states and receive a multi-year financial framework as a cost estimate. The purposes for which the funds are to be used are defined in the annual budget of the continental institutions in order to implement the projects.[171]

As long as the Ministry of Finance is not communitarised, the peoples of the Member States decide on the financial allocations for each ministry within the framework of their national

---

169 Ministry of Finance - 9.5 Budget vote
170 Ministry of Finance - 9.7 Audit Court, 9.1 Financial plans of the ministries, 9.5 Budget Vote
171 https://ec.europa.eu/info/strategy/eu-budget_de

budget votes, regardless of whether it is communitarised or not. A national budget vote is the process of determining state expenditure,[172] as well as budget negotiations in parliaments or bodies of the member states.

Once communitarised, the Ministry of Finance in the middle ring is given responsibility for fiscal policy in all member states. In the middle ring, all state revenues[173] are transferred to the continental Ministry of Finance and distributed in a continental budget vote[174] . The special feature in the middle ring is that the budgets of the member states remain separate. Each member state receives a state account at the continental People's Bank.[175] In the Continental Union budget vote, all Continental Union citizens are entitled to vote for all communitarised ministries in the middle ring. For all non-communitarised ministries, only those nationals of a Member State are entitled to vote.

In the inner ring, national financial policy is pursued, which is described in the Ministry of Finance.

6.4.10.4 debts

In the course of communitarisation, debts are reduced through taxes on assets.[176] In the outer ring, debts are still permitted that do not exceed the fixed admission criteria of the monetary union. Communitarisation into the middle ring may only be carried out by debt-free member states. For communitarisation into the inner ring, savings in the amount of the budget for the coming year are necessary.

6.4.10.4.1 Limitation of the debts

To limit the debts, a member state's budget may have a maximum deficit of 2% of its Gross Domestic Product and a maximum debt of a member state of 50% of its Gross

---

172 Ministry of Finance - 9 State expenditure
173 Ministry of Finance - 8 State revenues
174 Ministry of Finance - 9.5 Budget vote
175 Ministry of Finance - 11.7 State Account
176 Ministry of Finance - 5.4 Tax on assets

Domestic Product. All indebted member states must reduce their debts through debt conversion and debt reduction procedures.[177] If they do not achieve this, they must leave the common budget again.

6.4.10.4.2 State bankruptcies

The Continental Audit Court prepares and publishes reports on the granting and repayment of loans. In the course of communitarisation, the procedures of financial and burden equalisation as well as business cycle equalisation are used to avert state bankruptcy.[178] However, the people of the donor member states must agree to the procedures. If they refuse, the member state goes bankrupt and its creditors suffer a default on payment until the state is solvent again, but at the earliest after 10 years. Within this period, only barter trade may be conducted with the affected state so that it can build up a functioning domestic economy. The granting of loans to an insolvent state is inadmissible. Humanitarian aid and asylum remain permissible.

If states have become indebted by bailing out banks or companies, these banks or companies must repay the state aid money with interest. The interest rate corresponds to the inflation rate and does not apply in the case of deflation. The period is 10 years and can be extended up to 20 years, but this doubles the interest rate. The citizens have the right to reclaim their tax money immediately and must fulfil a veto quorum for this, which is followed by a committee and a voting. If the will of the people is confirmed, the payments become due immediately, together with the interest accrued to date. If the payments cannot be made in full, the affected banks or companies are immediately sold off in whole or in parts and all their assets are paid out to creditors and customers. Remaining amounts flow to the shareholders or other owners.

---

177 Ministry of Finance - 7.3 Debt conversion, 7.4 Debt reduction
178 Ministry of Finance – 7.1 Financial and burden equalisation, 7.5 Business cycle equalisation

6.4.11 Continental Union tax policy

In the course of the communitarisation of the Ministries of Finance, the tax system is simplified to such an extent that tax fraud becomes almost impossible and many rules become unnecessary.[179] The types of taxes and tax rates will be aligned with each other. The requirement is to retain only value added taxes, business taxes and tariffs and to split all other types of tax into one of these three tax types or abolish them. Taxes on assets are levied as long as the Continental Union or member states are in debt. Continental Union taxes on assets are collected on all debts of the Continental Union. Indebted member states levy taxes on assets in their country until they are debt-free.

6.4.11.1 Harmonised taxes

So-called direct taxes are managed exclusively by the member states. They are only harmonised in order to be able to exclude double taxation and tax avoidance in the internal market. These are mainly taxes that are incurred by companies. The business tax on the internal market of the Continental Union is a sales tax because all companies with locations in several Member States belong to the Free Market Economy.[180] The country-of-destination principle is applied without exception. For example, if subsidiaries operate in a Member State with higher business taxes, all inflows to the company account are taxed at that rate. After this tax deduction, subsidiaries can then pass on part of the profits to the parent company. This onward transfer must be made through the corporate tax accounts at People's Banks in both affected Member States.[181] As a result, payments from continental foreign countries are automatically recognised and not taxed when they are paid into the corporate account of the parent company.

A profit tax is only levied on Social Market Economy companies.[182] However, Social Market Economy companies

---

179 Ministry of Finance - 5 Tax policy
180 Ministry of Finance - 5.2.5 Sales tax
181 Ministry of Finance - 5.5.2 Corporate Tax Account
182 Ministry of Finance - 5.2.6 Profit tax

may only have subsidiaries in other Member States once the ministries for SEs in these Member States have been communitarised. Accordingly, the same Social Market Economy company tax rate applies in all Member States, together with uniform laws for Social Market Economy companies.

6.4.11.2 Uniform taxes

So-called indirect taxes are subject to the uniform tax law of the Continental Union and leave the member states certain leeway. These are predominantly taxes that are incurred by consumers. Value added tax is one of them. In the course of communitarisation, indirect taxes are completely standardised.[183] Excise duties on certain goods will be abolished and converted into fees that cover the costs incurred by the consumption of the goods.[184] Input tax deductions will no longer be necessary because value added tax will in future be deducted directly from the consumer and not from the entrepreneur. Refunds and tax exemptions will be abolished because the border crossing of property will not be taxed as long as no entrepreneurial intention is pursued with it. For entrepreneurial intentions, corporate tax law applies. Refunds to foreigners are eliminated because value added tax is levied as Customs on export.[185]

6.4.11.3 Tax administration

Continental tax administration is characterised by uniform procedures of the Tax Offices of all member states and culminates in the merger into a Continental Tax Office in the middle ring. The exchange of information is managed via a continental Tax Directory. Tax matters are handled by citizens and companies through their tax account at the People's Bank. The tax auditors of the Company Auditing Agency and

---

183 Ministry of Finance - 5.1 Value added tax
184 Ministry of Finance - 5.8 Tax reduction, Ministry of Health - 5.12.3 Addictive drugs Health Insurance
185 Ministry of Finance - 5.3 Tariffs

the Tax Investigation Department of Customs take over the control and collection of outstanding debts.[186]

6.4.12 Continental Union education policy

In the continental education policy, attendance at various educational institutions across the continent is made possible, as well as uniform degrees that are recognised in each Member State. Training is provided to Continental Union citizens of the domestic market, who have settled inland, in the educational institutions of the Ministry of Education. The Ministry of Education is responsible for respecting the capacity limits and restrictions for foreigners once the capacity limits of the educational institutions are reached.

6.4.12.1 Vocational education

In the course of communitarisation, the minimum requirements for vocational qualifications and the curricula are standardised.[187] In cooperation with the ministries for family, innovation, labour and economy, topics are defined that are covered in the curriculum and are part of the final examinations.[188] The order in which learners work on the contents and how teachers teach the individual contents is not specified. Only a methodological choice must be offered to learners so that they can adapt it to their learning style.[189] The final examinations are set centrally and are uniform in all educational institutions. Graduates thus prove their ability to master the following professional activities and to provide them in a similar quality. This is ensured by the Examinations Offices of the primary, comprehensive and higher education institutions. Colleges wishing to offer specialised or more

---

186 Ministry of Finance - 4 Tax Office, 5.6 Tax Directory, 5.5 Tax Account, 5.7 Company Auditing Agency Tax Auditor, Ministry of Security - 8.3 Tax Investigation Department
187 Ministry of Education - 4.4.2 Curriculum Development, 5.10.9.1 Curriculum Implementation
188 Ministry of Labour - 11.2 Vocational training
189 Ministry of Education - 5.11.2 Learning Type Test, 5.12.1 Hybrid Concept

general qualifications submit their concept to the responsible Examinations Office for approval. The qualifications to be examined are also standardised in colleges, but not the specific content of a final paper. This is to enable learners to choose their own research focus.

In the course of communitarisation, continental cooperation in vocational education and training is being expanded so that learners work with or in companies or do research to receive in-service training.[190]

6.4.12.2 Unified education area

In cooperation with the ministries of education and labour, the recognition of educational qualifications in the internal market is regulated. A lowering of educational standards is ruled out. The Ministry of Education offers a continental exchange programme for learners and ensures the recognition of qualifications.[191]

The workload for certificates and performance in examinations is measured uniformly.[192] In cooperation with the Ministry of Education, the Education and Examinations Offices[193] of all Member States are supported with methods of measurement to determine the learning content of a certificate. Certificates will be categorised according to subject area and degree.[194] Certificates will be standardised by making clear which topics of which subjects have been learnt by learners and to what extent.[195] Rigid timetables, time or subject requirements, sequences and modules for the acquisition of certificates will be abolished. Learners should decide for themselves when

---

190 Ministry of Education - 4.9 Education through work, 4.10 Education through research

191 Ministry of Education - 4.8.2 Foreigner recognition, 9.16 Foreign exchange, 11.6.5 International students

192 Ministry of Education - 9.2 certificates, 9.19 final examinations, 11.6.4.1 performance certificates, 11.6.4.2 seat certificates, 11.6.8 university degrees

193 Ministry of Education - 4.6 Examinations Office, 4.5 Education Authority

194 Ministry of Education - 8.7.4 Subjects, 9.15 School subjects, 11.1 Subject areas

195 Ministry of Education - 5.9 Education Directory

they learn which content an educational institution prescribes for the acquisition of a qualification. The move to a single education area will start in colleges and be extended to all comprehensive schools and primary schools in the Member States.

6.4.13 Continental Union Research Policy

The continental ministries of education, innovation and business coordinate continental cooperation between companies, state institutes, education and research institutions.[196] In the course of communitarisation, the research communities[197] are extended to all continental education and research institutions and coordinated via the continental Research Directory. Research results will be published there during ongoing studies and at the end. This makes the Research Directory the continental digital scientific journal.[198] All financial resources from the funds of the member states for the promotion of research and development will be transferred to open pots of the Research Cost Fund.[199]

6.4.14 Continental Union Innovation

In the Innovation Union, Member States pool their efforts to develop innovation. In the course of communitarisation, funding, searching for research areas, state research projects, cooperation partners, job advertisements, success stories, research infrastructure, project databases, regulations, statistics, industrial property rights and knowledge is facilitated in directories and databases. The Ministry of Innovation operates the Research Directory, the Ideas Directory and the Innovation Database for this purpose.[200] The Ministry of

196 Ministry of Education - 11.7.4 Research projects with companies, 11.7.2 State research institutes, 11.2 University, Ministry of Innovation - International cooperation, research institutions
197 Ministry of Education - 11.7.1 Research community
198 https://ec.europa.eu/info/research-and-innovation/strategy/goals-research-and-innovation-policy_de
199 Ministry of Innovation - 5.3.1 Research Cost Fund
200 Ministry of Innovation - 5.3 Research Directory, 8 Ideas Directory,

Labour operates the Labour Directory and the Success Model Directory and, with the Company Auditing Agency, ensures the necessary audits and commercialisation of innovations.[201] The Innovation Union focuses on inventive activity, protection of inventions and rapid and successful commercialisation. In the educational institutions, there are invention lessons and measures for education through research.[202] Outside educational institutions, the Ministry of Innovation provides measures for innovation through education and for innovation promotion.[203]

The Patent Offices of the member states merge to form a continental Patent Office.[204] The same happens with the patent courts. All regulations on industrial property rights are unified. The Innovation Union is completed when the ministries of education and innovation are communitarised in the middle ring. The state research projects[205] will be coordinated through continental cooperation based on the division of labour.[206][207]

6.4.15 Continental Union Digital Policy

Continental digital policy is characterised by a digitalised state administration, data security and citizen participation. The fact that there are hardly any ministries for digital affairs in the member states is used as an opportunity to build a continental Ministry of Digital Affairs. This Ministry of Digital Affairs unifies all digital-related laws and regulates the handling of the internet and companies with digital cross-border services.[208] The digital service and administers the security of digital

9.7 Innovation Database
201 Ministry of Labour - 13 Labour Directory, 20.9 Success Model Directory, 20.7.5 innovation auditor, 20.7.3 technical auditor, 20.7.4 technical auditor, 20.7.7 business consultant
202 Ministry of Education - 9.15.1.2 School subject in the sixth learning year: Inventing, 4.10 Education through research
203 Ministry of Innovation - 6 Innovation through Education, 9 Innovation Promotion
204 Ministry of Innovation - 7.3 Patent Office
205 Ministry of Innovation - 5.4 State research projects
206 Ministry of Innovation - 5.1 Continental Cooperation
207 https://ec.europa.eu/info/research-and-innovation/strategy_de
208 Ministry of Digital Affairs - 4 Digital law, 7 Digital data protection, 8 Digital crime, 9 Digital economy, 10 Internet

administration.[209] The Continental Statistical Office unifies data collection and brings together the data of all member states in the Continental Statistical System[210] . In the course of communitarisation, all Statistical Offices merge.[211] The Law Directory[212] is expanded continentally by making all laws of the Continental Union and its member states available and assessable. Users can participate interactively in the Legislative Directory[213] . Citizens of the Continental Union can also participate in continental politics at voting computers, in intranet cafés and via their personal People's Computers.[214] As part of the communitarisation, a state corporation is operated to provide the infrastructure and terminal devices for the continental intranet. [215]

6.4.16 Continental Union Media Policy

In the course of communitarisation, a continental News Television[216] is established and other TV channels are created, all of which are placed under the continental Ministry of Media Affairs. These new state TV channels emerge from all the public broadcasting authorities of the member states.[217] They will be divided into the eight different TV channels.[218] The citizens' television will be financed with funds for audiovisual works. Media law will be unified across the continent.[219]

209 Ministry of Digital Affairs - 2.1.2.1 Digital Service, 5 Digital Administration
210 https://ec.europa.eu/eurostat/de/web/european-statistical-system/overview
211 Ministry of Digital Affairs - 6 Statistical Office
212 Ministry of Justice - 4.7 Law Directory
213 Ministry of State Organisation - 9.10.6.1 Legislative Directory
214 Ministry of Digital Affairs - 11 Intranet, 11.1 Intranet Café, 12 Directories, 13.6 People's Computers, 14 Programmes, 15 Computer Games, Ministry of State Organisation - 7.1 Mediative
215 Ministry of Digital Affairs - 5 Digital Administration, 13 People's Innovation Company Intranet
216 Ministry of Media - 8 News Television
217 Ministry of Media Affairs - 5 State broadcasting
218 Ministry of Media - 7 Government Television, 8 News Television, 9 Local Television, 10 Party Television, 11 Nationwide Citizen Television, 12 Surveillance Television, 13 Educational Television, 14 Youth Television
219 Ministry of Media Affairs - 4 Media Law

As with the Ministry of Digital Affairs, there are no comparable media ministries in the member states. With the help of the Ministry of Digital Affairs and the Ministry of Media Affairs, the mediative[220] is being imported as a fourth democratically controlled state power.

6.4.17 Continental Union family policy

Continental family policy unifies rules on marriage, parenting, children, youths, culture, sports, inheritance, equality and human rights. The communitarisation in the Ministry of Family Affairs is adapted to the speed of integration of the member states as far as the ideas of marriage and partnership are concerned.

6.4.17.1 Family

In the course of communitarisation, the law on partnering, marriage contracts, senior citizens, death and Registry Offices will be unified.[221] In matters of parenting, common guidelines are agreed for the continental introduction of the parenting licence, as well as for uniform requirements for Youth Welfare Offices and options in the case of wanting children.[222] The Family Directory becomes available continent-wide and the Institute for Family Research expands its field of research accordingly.[223] The Ministry of Family Affairs is responsible for the formulation of continentally recognised manners and the promotion of democracy.[224]

---

220 Ministry of State Organisation - 7.1 Mediative

221 Ministry of Family Affairs - 6 Registry Office, 7.3 Partnering, 7.4.1 Marriage contract, 10 Senior citizens, 11 Death

222 Ministry of Family Affairs - 7.5 Child Welfare, 7.6 Youth Welfare Office, 7.7 Parenting

223 Ministry of Family Affairs - 7.2 Family Directory, 7.1 Institute for Family Research

224 Ministry of Family Affairs - 4 manners, 5 promotion of democracy

6.4.17.2 Children

Children's rights[225] will quickly become fundamental rights for children, which will be treated with the same attention as the observance of other fundamental rights. In the course of communitarisation, a uniform age of majority will be established and child benefits of the same amount across the continent will be paid out on the child ID card and tied to uniform purposes.[226] In the course of communitarisation, the Youth Alliance becomes active throughout the continent and youth centres offer the same services everywhere.[227]

6.4.17.3 Culture

In the course of communitarisation, the promotion of elites is restricted in favour of the broad mass of the population. Only Olympic Games are promoted with their sporting disciplines in top-level sport. Museums with art treasures are sold to run or support recreational facilities for art, music, sports and to offer events and playgrounds for young and old. Clubs and honorary services are supported.[228]

6.4.18 Continental Union infrastructure policy

The communitarisation of continental infrastructure policy takes place in the areas of raw materials, urban and rural development, waste management, construction, networks, digital infrastructure, transport and energy. The State Utilities, Traffic Office and Building Office take care of the construction, administration and innovative renewal of the infrastructure.[229]

---

225 Ministry of Family Affairs - 8.1 Children's rights
226 Ministry of Family Affairs - 8.3 Child ID card, 8.4 Child benefit, 8.7 Age of majority
227 Ministry of Family Affairs - 8.5 Youths
228 Ministry of Family Affairs - 9 Leisure
229 Ministry of Infrastructure - 4.8 State Utilities, 8.3 Traffic Office, 5.1 Building Office

6.4.18.1 Raw materials

The continental raw materials policy focuses on a common strategy for the use and support of raw materials. Parts of the strategy are the supply of the Continental Union and the world market as well as a more effective and economical use of raw materials and the development of a circular economy.[230] In the course of communitarisation, the supply of the member states is supported before the supply of the world market. Raw materials that have to be imported from third countries will be replaced by innovations so that the continent becomes independent of raw material imports. The long-term goal is regional and continental self-sufficiency, so that sufficient raw materials are available worldwide because production methods are being changed to regional and organic production.[231]

6.4.18.2 Spatial development

For the continental spatial development policy, common regulations are issued for homeland protection, urban development, recreation and the administration of state buildings.[232] The aim of spatial development is to make state green spaces agriculturally and playfully usable for citizens. The Real Estate Directory is extended to the entire continent.[233] In the course of communitarisation, all building regulations are first standardised and state buildings and residential buildings are constructed with the help of a continental construction team.[234]

Waste management is communitarised as part of environmental policy and consists of requirements to dispose of different types of waste[235] and landfill[236] . In the course of communitarisation,

---

230https://eur-lex.europa.eu/legal-content/DE/TXT/?uri=LEGISSUM
%3A24040103_1&qid=1620168698223
231 Ministry of Infrastructure - 4.3 Raw materials
232 Ministry of Infrastructure - 4.1 Homeland Protection, 4.4 Urban
Development, 4.6 Leisure, 4.7 Facilities Management
233 Ministry of Infrastructure - 4.3.2 Agricultural Land, 4.5 Real Estate
Directory
234 Ministry of Infrastructure - 5 Building
235https://eur-lex.europa.eu/summary/chapter/2017.html
236https://eur-lex.europa.eu/legal-content/DE/

waste is reduced or recycled because producers have to add disposal costs to the price in order to finance the facilities for landfill or waste recycling.[237]

6.4.18.3 Traffic

Continental transport policy is driven by the communitarisation of infrastructure ministries. Space transport is managed by international or continental space agencies. They ensure the establishment of spaceports and the approval of means of transport and the disposal of space debris. The Global Navigation Satellite System is being expanded to enable automated individual transport in the air.[238]

In the course of communitarisation, the laws and networks for transport are being unified.[239] In order to protect the environment and increase efficiency, the continental shift to new means of transport is being promoted. Individual transport is being shifted to new types of bicycles for local transport and to flying cars for long-distance transport. The People's Innovation Company Intranet provides the necessary digital infrastructure.[240] A continental air traffic control system controls the continental airspace. Long-distance roads are dismantled and no longer built, fine dust and tyre wear are eliminated. Public transport will be transferred to above-ground and underground maglev trains. Tracks will be dismantled, noise and abrasion will be eliminated. Intercontinental traffic is shifted to the stratosphere, interstellar traffic is built up. Travel times are shortened and new planets can be explored and colonised. Oceans and rivers continue to be used as waterways. Vehicles use new technologies, run on renewable energy and are monitored for water protection.

TXT/?uri=legissum%3Al21208
237 Ministry of Infrastructure - 4.9.2 Waste disposal
238 Ministry of Infrastructure - 8.10.1 Airspace
239 Ministry of Infrastructure - 8 Traffic
240 Ministry of Infrastructure - 8.10.1 Airspace, Ministry of Digital Affairs - 13 People's Innovation Company Intranet

6.4.18.4 Energy

Continental energy policy concerns the coordination of the continental energy transition and includes the continental emissions trading system for financing and standards for environmental sustainability and security of supply.[241] In the course of communitarisation, the underground networks will be connected to exchange and store continentally generated energy.[242] Centralised power plants will be instituted at all suitable locations in the Continental Union, and decentralised plants for municipal and private self-sufficiency. Expenditure on research and development of new energy sources will be pooled.[243] Waste disposal, treatment and recycling will be included as part of the energy policy. A continental circular economy for waste will be established as part of the communitarisation. All disposal costs will be shifted to producers, making products with a better possibility to be recycled or repaired cheaper.[244]

6.4.19 Continental Union Health Policy

The continental health policy includes uniform requirements for medicines, nutrition, exercise, drugs, diseases, vaccines, risk assessment, occupational safety, environmental protection, healthcare systems, billing and documentation of medical services, as well as health safety and public health measures.[245] The scientific determination of requirements is carried out by the institutes of the Ministry of Health in cooperation with state education and research institutions.

The Health Card and the Health Directory are used

---

241 Ministry of Infrastructure - 9.5 Energy transformation, 9.2 Economic efficiency, 9.3 Environmental sustainability, 9.4 Energy consumption

242 Ministry of Infrastructure - 6.2 Underground networks, 9.6 Energy Directory, 9.1 Security of supply

243 Ministry of Infrastructure - 9.7 Energy supply, 9.8 Development of new power sources

244 Ministry of Infrastructure - 4.9.1 Water Supply, 4.9.2 Waste disposal

245 Ministry of Health - 5.9 Medicines, 6.1 Nutrition, 6.2 Exercise, 5.11 Drugs, 4.5 Institutes of the Ministry of Health, 5 Health care, 4 Healthcare system, Ministry of Labour - 14.2 Occupational safety and health, 14.3 Environmental protection

continentally. Country-specific health profiles are automatically created via the Health Directory. They also provide information on which citizens are sick or healthy and where. The continental Health Card enables patients to be treated everywhere with their health insurance of a Member State. All requirements for physicians, pharmacists, health care facilities, care and the pharmaceutical industry will be standardised.[246] The requirements are checked by the health auditors of the Company Auditing Agency.[247] As part of the communitarisation, drugs are legalised and continental health care funds are established for general health care, addictive drugs, and immortality.

6.4.19.1 Product safety

For product safety, the ministries of health and labour share responsibilities between health safety assessment and consumer protection.[248]
Common measures in the field of food hygiene, contamination and the spread of pests or diseases are implemented uniformly by the Health Agencies. State services include training, a rapid alert system, a tracking system, a pesticide database and a reporting system.
In the course of communitarisation, food safety is the responsibility of the ministries of health and labour.[249] The requirements on sustainable use of nature provide for the replacement of chemicals and medicines and uniform rules for the use of genetic engineering.[250]

---

246 Ministry of Health - 5.11 Drugs, 5.12 Health Insurance, 5.2 Health Card, 5.3 Health Directory, 5.4 Physicians, 5.8 Pharmacists, 5.6 Health Facilities, 5.7 Care, 5.10 Pharmaceutical Industry
247 Ministry of Labour - 20.7.2 Health auditor
248 Ministry of Health - 6.4 Product safety, Ministry of Labour - 17 Consumer protection, 20.7.2 Health auditor, 20.7.4 Technical auditor
249 Ministry of Health - 6.3 Food Safety, Ministry of Labour - 19.5 Food Quality, 19.13 Food Directory, 19.8 Food Industry
250 Ministry of Health - 4.1 Health Agency, 6.5 Sustainable Use of Nature

6.4.19.2 Environmental protection

Numerous agreements on environmental protection exist within the framework of international cooperation.[251] Environmental crime is punished by criminal law and prevented by preventive law.[252] The polluter pays principle applies, according to which originators are liable for their environmental damage. The precautionary principle refuses or withdraws authorisation as a precautionary measure if a risk to humans and the environment cannot be ruled out due to insufficient data. To satisfy both principles, a great deal of data is collected and evaluated so that conditions can be clarified and plans and programmes can be checked for their environmental compatibility.[253]

In the course of communitarisation, environmental policy becomes part of health prevention.[254] The two principles and many environmental protection standards are adopted. Regularisation is reduced through simple laws for producers and disposers of pollution and made unnecessary through innovation.

6.4.19.2.1 Common tools and agencies

In the course of communitarisation, emissions trading is replaced by measures that are financed by pricing in the costs of pollution.[255] The health auditors and innovation auditors audit and certify companies with environmentally sound working practices.[256] The Health Agencies ensure compliance with the standards and receive scientific support from the Institute of Environmental Medicine.[257] The Environment Directory becomes a continental register of pollutant releases

---

251 https://eur-lex.europa.eu/summary/chapter/2024.html
252 https://eur-lex.europa.eu/summary/chapter/2023.html
253 https://eur-lex.europa.eu/summary/chapter/2022.html
254 Ministry of Health - 6 Health prevention
255 Ministry of Infrastructure - 9.5 Energy transformation, 10.1 Emissions trading, 4.9.2.1 Pricing in pollution costs
256 Ministry of Labour - 20.7.2.2 Environmental audit, 20.7.5.1 Innovation audit
257 Ministry of Health - 4.1 Health Agency, 4.5.4 Institute of Environmental Health

and transfers and an information platform on observations of the state of the environment.

6.4.19.2.2 Common standards and measures

The existing requirements for environmental protection are supplemented or replaced by the standards and measures of the ministries of health, infrastructure, labour, innovation and justice and harmonised across the continent. The Ministry of Health takes responsibility for this and sets its own requirements regarding circular economy, sustainable use of nature and environmental protection.[258] The Ministry of Infrastructure contributes through environmentally friendly requirements in the areas of transport, energy, homeland and construction.[259] The Ministry of Labour contributes through requirements, audits and innovations in the areas of enterprise policy, consumer protection, agriculture and auditing by the Company Auditing Agency.[260] The Ministry of Innovation contributes through state research projects, the Institute of Technology and Environmental Innovation Cartels.[261] The Ministry of Justice contributes through consideration of environmental damage in court proceedings, compensation for victims of pollution, imprisonment for pollution linked to the duration of the natural degradation process, sentences for dragging out environmental innovation and creating negative

---

258 Ministry of Health - 6.7.2.1 Circular economy, 6.5 Sustainable use of nature, 6.6 Environmental protection
259 Ministry of Infrastructure - 4.2 Environmental protection, 4.3 Raw materials, 4.3.2 Agricultural land, 4.9.1 Water supply, 4.9.2 Waste disposal, 5.3.1 Energy efficiency, 5.12 Building materials, 8.4 Environmental protection in transport, 9.3 Environmental compatibility, 9.4 Energy consumption, 9.5 Energy transformation
260 Ministry of Labour - 14.3 Environmental protection, 14.4 Circular economy, 14.5 Packaging, 14.6 Certificates against negative externalities, 17.7.5 Environmental traffic lights, 19.8.3 Sustainability, 19.8.4 Climate protection, 19.8.5 Production security despite climate impacts, 19.9 Forest, hunting and forestry policy, 19.10 Fisheries policy, 19.4 Company Auditing Agency audits in agriculture, 20.7.3.5.9 Prevention of waste, 20.7.3.7.2 Audit of the environmental impact
261 Ministry of Innovation - 5.4.1 Providing for the Future, 5.4.2 Digital Transformation, 5.4.4 Transport Transformation, 7.1 Institute of Technology, 9.10.3 Environmental Innovation

externalities, and special sentences for pollution in Barter Economy Zones.[262]

6.4.20 Continental Union security policy

The continental security policy first unifies the rules on security policy and enables police, Customs and military cooperation between member states. In the course of communitarisation in the middle ring, common agencies are created.

6.4.20.1 Defence

Defence policy is the responsibility of the Ministry of Security[263] and is supported by the Ministry of Foreign Affairs at the continental level in defence integration. For continental defence, the armies of the member states initially switch from attack to defence of national borders. In the course of communitarisation, a Continental Defence Army is being built up[264] . The Continental Defence Army defends only the member states and the territory of the Continental Union. All military and civilian operations in third countries are discontinued. All member states ally their armies to form the Continental Defence Army. The best weapon systems remain and the best troops remain soldiers. All other war weapons will be stored or converted so that they can be used for civilian purposes in the civil service[265] and will only be converted again in the event of war. The soldiers will be integrated into the other services of the Ministry of Security, will continue to receive ongoing training in defence tactics and will only be deployed as soldiers in the event of war. The defence budgets of all member states will be merged and gradually reduced. The surpluses due to falling expenditure in the barracks and in

---

262 Ministry of Justice - 5.8 Assessment of damage, 8.2.2 International economic law, 8.6.1 Environmental pollution, 8.8.3 Procrastination of innovation, 8.11.6 Negative externalities, 8.15.1 Environmental pollution in the Barter Economy
263 Ministry of Security - 9 Military
264 Ministry of Safety - 9.3.1 Continental Defence Army
265 Ministry of Infrastructure - 5.8 Construction Team, Ministry of Planned Economy - 9.4.1 Social Service

military pay will be used in the short term to set up a defence shield of missiles and laser weapons covering the territory of all Continental Defence Army member states, similar to the Iron Dome[266] in Israel. In addition, member states are creating land-based hidden defences against ground forces and weapon systems against ships and submarines on the coasts.

Combat missions of the Continental Defence Army may only serve the purpose of averting a direct war of aggression against member states of the Continental Defence Army. So-called foreign missions or assistance missions of continental soldiers, regardless of whether they are conducted by a member state or a military alliance, will be terminated immediately and are prohibited thereafter. The Continental Defence Army joins a global defence alliance, which should also include all nuclear powers.

6.4.20.2 Crime

To combat continental crime, security policy is unified. Police authorities work according to uniform requirements and merge into a continental police force. Terrorism will be dealt with through export bans on weapons, withdrawal of continental military units from third countries, international neutrality, participation and demarcation. Preventive measures for the control of weapons and explosives remain in place. Drug trafficking no longer plays a role due to legalisation.

In the course of communitarisation, the People's Protection Service, Police, Customs and Military take over the training of their personnel according to uniform requirements in cooperation with the Ministry of Education[267] . In the outer ring, the continental police becomes responsible as soon as a crime becomes cross-border and leads the searches and investigations of this case in all member states. Once the Ministry of Security is communitarised, in the middle ring, the continental police become the police of the member states. The People's Protection Service will be approved continentally

---

266https://de.wikipedia.org/wiki/Iron_Dome
267Ministry of Education - 2.1.1.1 Education and training for the state service

to approve the police, give soldiers a job in peacetime, undertake social missions and replace all private security companies.[268] The continental secret service will be established to combat attacks by other secret services and organised crime. Cooperation and data exchange between police stations and public prosecutors' offices will be digitalised through the Security Directory and the Investigation Directory.[269]

6.4.20.3 Disaster management

Within the framework of communitarisation in disaster management, humanitarian aid is divided. All preventive protection measures and post-disaster assistance for disasters caused by nature or humans will become part of disaster management in the Ministry of Security.[270] In the course of communitarisation, the entire prevention of danger is unified and extended to the entire continent.[271] Humanitarian aid provided as development aid by the Continental Union becomes part of the area of accountability of development aid and is rotated around the continent and neighbouring developing countries. Humanitarian aid under the United Nations remains and is used in international disaster management.[272]

6.4.20.4 Border Guard

In the course of communitarisation, a continental border protection policy is introduced. All persons without a valid entry document will be turned away at the border. The aim is that asylum applications and entry requests will only be made in embassies outside the Continental Union. This will make any journeys for illegal entry into the Continental Union unnecessary, as they will be punishable by refoulement

268 Ministry of Security - 4 Security Policy, 7 Police, 4.11 Terrorism, 6 People's Protection Service
269 Ministry of Security - 9.3.2 Continental Secret Service, 4.6 Security Directory, 7.4 Investigation Directory
270 Ministry of Security - 5.7 Disaster management
271 Ministry of Security - 5 Prevention of danger
272 Ministry of Security - 5.7.9 International disaster management

or detention and will in no way allow free residence in the Continental Union. The quotas, which Member States determine through their quotas of foreigners, give embassies clear requirements as to when, where and how much immigration is possible. The Customs of all member states initially receive uniform regulations and later become a continental Customs.[273] It staffs border posts for controls and monitors border areas with the help of the military. Security forces are sent from all member states for the joint protection of the Continental Union's external borders.

6.4.20.5 Travel data systems

Travel data is collected, stored and shared according to uniform requirements. Upon entry and departure, data on identity, biometrics, date, time and place of entry and departure are collected and stored. Carriers are obliged to report personal data of the persons they carry into the Continental Union from third countries. Failure to comply with this obligation will result in fines, confiscation of the means of transport and withdrawal of the company's authorisation to transport in the Continental Union.

In the course of communitarisation, travel data on border crossing and residence permits are stored in the continental Travel Directory. Data on residence permits provide information on the period of validity, extension, revocation and cancellation of visas and their holders or applicants in order to avoid multiple visas in different Member States. The Continental Investigation Directory[274] stores data on witnesses, wanted and convicted criminals, illegal immigrants and missing persons, as well as corresponding objects from Member States or third countries that are wanted or whose border crossing into or out of the Continental Union is to be prevented. Fingerprint data of asylum applicants and asylum applications are stored in the continental Asylum Directory[275] . All directories will be integrated into one search portal. The

---

273 Ministry of Security - 8 Customs
274 Ministry of Security - 7.4 Investigation Directory
275 Ministry of Integration - 8.3 Asylum Directory

authorities for security and justice of all Member States can access it and enter their information there.

6.4.21 Continental Union Customs Union

Through the Customs Union, all Member States' customs authorities work together as one agency and abide by uniform rules. They protect consumers and the environment from harmful or counterfeit imports and illegal trade in endangered animal and plant species through customs controls at the external borders. Through a customs information system[276] , customs authorities provide mutual administrative assistance to exchange data on the movement of goods between Continental Union member states and third countries, and applicable regulations for the relevant foreign trade are automatically linked. Cash and protected intellectual property are specially controlled to prevent money laundering and counterfeiting. The legalisation of drugs will eliminate Customs' responsibilities in this area in the course of communitarisation.

In the course of communitarisation, tariffs are introduced within the Continental Union in order to bring living standards into line with each other as quickly as possible without lowering living standards in one member state. [277]

All uniform customs tariffs are included in the Tax Directory and linked to the regulations from the Law Directory.[278]

Customs exemptions apply to goods crossing the external borders of the Continental Union as part of a move, marriage, inheritance or in travellers' luggage and may be revoked in the event of a poor budgetary situation. Customs controls are carried out by customs officers at the borders and investigative activities are carried out by the Tax Investigation Department.[279]

---

276 https://eur-lex.europa.eu/legal-content/DE/
TXT/?uri=legissum%3Al11037
277 Ministry of Finance - 5.3 Tariffs
278 Ministry of Finance - 5.6 Tax Directory, Ministry of Justice - 4.7 Law Directory
279 Ministry of Security - 8.2 Border Protection, 8.3 Tax Investigation Department

6.4.22 Continental Union Justice Policy

Continental justice policy gives all citizens of the Continental Union the same fundamental rights, as well as many laws in cross-border civil and criminal law. Continental civil law regulates continental commercial transactions, insolvency proceedings, marriages, divorces, parental responsibility for their children, division of property and debt relationships. Cooperation between member states means that evidence is taken and documents are transmitted across borders. It is regulated which law of the Member States is to be applied in an individual case. Admission to courts will be digitalised.

In continental criminal law, the continental prosecution and sentencing of offenders, as well as the compensation of victims, are regulated uniformly. Data on wanted and convicted offenders from member states and third countries are exchanged via an information system. Offenders and victims have the same rights to information, presence at the negotiation, presumption of innocence, interpretation, legal assistance and victim protection in each Member State. Whistleblowers who publish violations of Continental Union law are protected. Judicial decisions, sentences or monetary fines are recognised by all member states. Extradition procedures are facilitated through the continental arrest warrant. War crimes are uniformly defined as such and prosecuted under criminal law. Agreements on mutual legal assistance and extradition are agreed with third countries.[280]

In the course of communitarisation, continental jurisdiction and law enforcement will become responsible for an increasing number of legal forms because all laws will be aligned with each other. With communitarisation, clemency law and forms of punishment are also aligned and implemented together.[281]

---

280 https://eur-lex.europa.eu/summary/chapter/2303.html
281 Ministry of Justice - 4.8 areas of law, 6 clemency law, 7 forms of punishment

6.4.22.1 Continental judicial authorities

In the course of communitarisation, a continental public prosecutor's office is established to investigate, prosecute and charge offences that have a cross-border character. It coordinates the cooperation of the judicial authorities of the member states and ensures that judicial decisions taken in one member state are also recognised and enforced in every other member state. It is responsible in the outer ring as soon as cross-border investigative work becomes necessary and directs the investigation of this case in all member states. In case of doubt, it decides on the place of jurisdiction and sends the results of the investigation to the responsible court. Once communitarised, the Ministry of Justice becomes part of the prosecution service in the middle ring in the Member States and uses the Court Directory to exchange data. The courts and court proceedings in the Member States will be unified in all instances and chambers.

The Continental Court is responsible for actions brought by organs of the Continental Union, private individuals and member states. It replaces the National Court of Justice in the middle ring. Lastly, the Constitutional Court will be communitarised, which means that the Constitutional Courts of the Member States will cease their service and a Constitutional Court will look after the Constitution of the United States of the Continent. With the communitarisation of the ministries of justice and security, the continental prosecutor's office becomes responsible for an increasing number of areas until it becomes the prosecutor's office of the continental courts.[282]

6.4.22.2 Fundamental rights

In order to standardise fundamental rights, human rights are taken as a model.[283] This regulates uniformly which dignity, freedoms, equality, solidarity, civil rights and rights must be respected in court proceedings. All authorities and institutions

---

282 Ministry of Justice - 5 court proceedings
283 https://europa.eu/european-union/topics/human-rights_de

of the Continental Union as well as all member states are obliged to comply. Exceptions are possible according to the principle of subsidiarity. In the course of communitarisation, the Federal Moderator's Office[284] becomes responsible for the observance of human rights by all state organs. The Ministry of State Organisation becomes responsible for all political and national rights.[285] All ministries implement the fundamental rights and enact criminal law that names and punishes violations. The Ministry of Justice guarantees Continental Union citizens the rule of law.[286]

6.4.22.3 Corruption

The continental policy against corruption and fraud includes state authorities and private companies or persons. In the course of communitarisation, the audit services of the ministries of media, justice, finance, labour, state organisation are unified.[287] They are responsible for quality management in state agencies, evaluation of work performance, revenues and expenditures, as well as prevention of corruption, protection against sabotage and, if necessary, disciplinary matters. Responsible for corruption in persons and organisations is the continental police and public prosecutor's office. The requirements of the Ministry of Justice against corruption, bribery and fraud are adopted accordingly.[288]

6.4.23 Continental Union Integration Policy

Continental integration policy covers the areas of free movement of persons, asylum, immigration, emigration and continental citizenship. In the course of communitarisation,

---

284 Ministry of State Organisation - 4.4 Federal Moderator's Office
285 Ministry of State Organisation - 8.1 Nationals
286 Ministry of Justice - 8 criminal law of the ministries, 4 principles of the rule of law
287 Ministries of media, justice, finance, labour, state organisation - 2.1.2.1 Audit services
288 Ministry of Justice - 4.6.7 Administrative instructions, 8.11.3 Judicial criminal law, 8.14.4 Non-transparent lobbying, 8.1.2 Bribery, 8.14.3 Bribery of state employees, 8.5.3 Insurance, 8.16.2 Social fraud

the policy for integration, immigration and asylum is the responsibility of the Ministry of Integration[289] and is supported by the Ministry of Foreign Affairs with procedures for granting visas and asylum applicants. The rules are being harmonised and procedures are being voted on by the authorities in the member states.

6.4.23.1 State communitarisation

Continental integration aims to enable a secure and free life in the long term. With policy integration through communitarisation of member states and accession countries, the economies of scale and production processes based on division of labour of internationalisation are used. The disadvantages of globalisation, such as tax havens, international anarchy without worldwide laws, police and justice, economic exploitation through different living standards, violation of environmental and occupational safety standards, immigration and emigration out of need, poverty and despair, instead of love for the country and its people, are avoided through borders. To make all peoples of the continent one people, commonalities are to be found and promoted. Divisive influences from governments and foreigners outside the continent are avoided and reduced.

6.4.23.2 Cultural integration

Cultural communitarisation is decoupled from state communitarisation in order to accommodate different speeds of integration. This is ensured by the similar cultural sphere across the continent. Divisive influences of religions are reduced through requirements and understanding. The predominant religion in the continent is considered the historically developed guiding religion of continental laws. The primary task of cultural integration in the short term is the harmonisation of the beliefs of the different or same religions. All other religions may continue to exist as long as they do

---

289 Ministry of Integration - 7 Immigration, 8 Asylum

not divide society or incite sections of the population.[290] What humans believe in is up to them. How humans display their faith in public and working hours or publicly propagate it through places of worship is limited by law. This limitation is set by the continental ministries of integration.

6.4.23.3 State documents for citizens

In the course of communitarisation, all state documents from the member states will be recognised and the requirements for the necessary content and their legal effects will be standardised. The Residents' Registration Office will be responsible for the recognition of documents.[291] To this end, it works together with the responsible embassy and agency.

6.4.23.4 Legal immigration

For a continental immigration policy, identity cards and immigration procedures are standardised. Personal and biometric details of the holders, method of production and security features are the same no matter where the immigration document or identity card is issued. Information on asylum, immigration and emigration is collected in the Asylum Directory, Travel Directory and Persons Directory and shared with Continental Union institutions and Member States.[292] Third-country nationals residing in the Continental Union are granted residence permits as long as they can adequately support and insure themselves and their dependents, they remain unpunished, they have been successfully naturalised and there is sufficient capacity in the quota of foreigners.[293]

---

290 Ministry of Integration - 6.5 Religion Management
291 Ministry of Integration - 4.4 Residents' Registration Office
292 Ministry of Integration - 8.3 Asylum Directory, Ministry of State Organisation - 4.6 Persons Directory
293 Ministry of Integration - 4.2.3 Naturalised persons, 7.4 Quota of foreigners, 7.5 Immigration conditions, 7.9 Departure procedure

6.4.23.4.1 Freedom of movement for Continental Union citizens

All Continental Union citizens enjoy the right of residence in all Member States as long as they have the nationality of a Member State. This means that they can travel to any Member State with their identity card or passport. They can stay there for up to three months without having to re-register. The only exceptions are for students, pensioners or unpaid workers who can adequately support and insure themselves and their dependents.

In the course of communitarisation on the outer ring, member states can impose requirements that restrict freedom of movement. In order to promote the integration of moving Continental Union citizens, the same immigration procedures and integration measures are offered to them as to other foreigners and nationals. They can use the Integration Directory and, if necessary, be forced to leave the country if they become criminals. As long as the social systems are not communitarised, they must also depart if they become insolvent.[294]

6.4.23.4.2 Continental identity cards

Identity cards for Continental Union citizens and residence documents for third-country nationals will be standardised. This includes uniform information, dimensions, layout, validity periods and a storage medium that can be read by machines. In the course of communitarisation, the identity cards of all Member States will be increasingly standardised until there is only one uniform identity card and passport for all Continental Union citizens.[295]

---

294 Ministry of Integration - 7 Immigration
295 Ministry of Integration - 4.4.1 Identity cards

6.4.23.4.3 Continental visas

Member States' passports and travel documents have digital storage media containing biometric data consisting of the face and two fingerprints. The data can be stored and read in a uniform form.[296] To make it easier to detect forged and genuine documents, the Investigation Directory has information on forged and genuine documents of the member states. Common standards for state documents and characteristics of detected forgeries are also stored there.

It is uniformly regulated for which third countries a visa requirement exists, according to which procedures visas are applied for and approved, where the visas are valid and how they are stored in the travel document. In agreements with third countries, exemptions and facilitations from the visa requirement are agreed.[297]

In the course of communitarisation, visas are issued in the embassies of the Continental Union according to uniform requirements and conditions if the quotas of foreigners[298] for third-country nationals are not exceeded.

6.4.23.4.4 Family reunification

In the course of communitarisation, family reunification is only possible for third-country nationals if they have already been naturalised, earn enough money to support and insure all family members, the quota of foreigners has not yet been met and if the family members have been naturalised within 5 years. The family members consist of spouses, children and non-marital partners. Otherwise, the rules of the ministries for Free Market Economy and Integration apply.[299]

---

296 https://eur-lex.europa.eu/legal-content/DE/
TXT/?uri=legissum%3Al14154
297 https://eur-lex.europa.eu/legal-content/DE/
TXT/?uri=legissum%3A4384449 https://eur-lex.europa.eu/legal-content/DE/TXT/?uri=legissum%3A4394574
298 Ministry of Integration - 7.4 Quota of foreigners
299 Ministry of Free Market Economy - 12.2.5 Family reunification, Ministry of Integration - 7.4.3 Following measures

6.4.23.4.5 Continental guest work

Third-country nationals receive a temporary residence permit linked to the duration of their research, training, studies, internship, voluntary service and au pair activity. Seasonal workers from third countries receive seasonal residence permits linked to their employment contracts. Skilled workers receive a temporary residence permit when there are no more corresponding skilled workers from member states looking for work. All third-country workers receive a combined residence and work permit, provided they can adequately support and insure themselves and their dependents and remain exempt from prosecution.

In the course of communitarisation, guest workers are paid more than domestic workers. The wage premium corresponds to the unemployment rate in the member state. When there is full employment, guest workers are paid less. In general, the quota of foreigners also applies to guest workers as a prerequisite for immigration, as well as full employment in the Continental Union.[300]

6.4.23.4.6 Continental asylum

Continental asylum policy creates common norms and procedures for asylum seekers. Common norms for recognising refugees and stateless persons as asylum seekers, are laid down as minimum standards in the Geneva Convention on Refugees.[301] In the course of communitarisation, refugees may not be used to prevent full employment, but may work as asylum seekers in their own economic cycle. Asylum applicants will only be able to apply at the embassies of the affected third countries or neighbouring countries directly adjacent to them. The legal process will be excluded. All other existing benefits for asylum applicants will be discontinued and invested in the construction of Asylum Villages in the Continental Union, where housing will be needed in the future. Responsibility

---

300 Ministry of Labour - 16.11 Guest work, Ministry of Integration - 7.5.2 Guest work
301 https://www.unhcr.org/dach/wp-content/uploads/sites/27/2017/03/ GFK_Pocket_2015_RZ_final_ansicht.pdf

for the asylum application procedure will be handed over to the ministries abroad and implementation to the embassies, which will cooperate with the Integration Agencies of the member states. The integration ministries of the member states are responsible for the release of reception capacities and for the stay of the asylum seekers in the member state.[302]

6.4.23.5 Illegal immigration

For continental management of immigration, the immigration authorities of the member states network with each other. They exchange information and offer joint training. To prevent illegal immigration, information is collected and shared on migration routes, identity card forgery, criminals and smuggling. To facilitate return, readmission agreements are made with third countries.

Border protection is strengthened and, if necessary, enforced with coercive measures. In the course of communitarisation, refugees transported from a third country to the external borders of the Continental Defence Army are considered an act of war, which can be punished with foreign trade sanctions against the affected state or a declaration of war by the Continental Defence Army.

In the course of communitarisation, the continental Integration Agency in the middle ring replaces the national Integration Agencies. Illegal immigrants are turned away at the border and, if necessary, also with coercive measures. Entry into the Continental Union is only possible if an embassy of a member state or the continental Ministry of Foreign Affairs has granted permission. Authorisation can be blanket for nationals of a third country with which a corresponding agreement exists, through a visa or an approved asylum application.

Illegal border crossing becomes a criminal offence punishable by 10 years detention, plus possible rescue costs. Detention is followed by deportation and a lifetime ban on entering the Continental Union. Those who disregard this entry ban are newly liable for a criminal offence and will be in detention for 5 years longer. In detention, illegal immigrants, like all

---

302Ministry of Integration - 8 Asylum

prisoners, receive no income and work as compensation for their crime on the peoples of the continent.[303]

6.4.23.5.1 Smugglers

Aiding and abetting illegal immigration, So-called smuggling of migrants, is prevented by a uniform definition of smuggling, criminal offences, responsible courts, responsible companies and sentences.[304] Accordingly, carriers can be fined for transporting illegal immigrants, lose means of transport through confiscation, receive occupational bans or responsible foreigners can be deported.[305]

In the course of communitarisation, smuggling is curbed by making all possibilities for legal immigration from third countries only possible in the embassy of a member state where the language of the applicant is spoken. The embassies provide transport services.

6.4.23.5.2 Employment of illegal immigrants

Employers of third-country nationals have the obligation to check their residence permit, keep a copy of the relevant document and notify the national authorities. Employers who do not comply have to pay monetary fines and repatriation, are excluded from state subsidies or have to pay them back. Criminal offences are committed if the violation is repeated, many illegal immigrants, minors or victims of trafficking are employed or exploited. Illegally employed persons have the possibility to file a complaint with a state agency against their employer, who will then be investigated.[306] In the course of communitarisation, the Company Auditing Agency checks whether all requirements for the legal employment of guest

303 Ministry of Justice - 8.9.5 Failure to comply with entry ban, 7.5 Detention
304 https://eur-lex.europa.eu/legal-content/DE/TXT/?uri=legissum%3A4362880
305 https://eur-lex.europa.eu/legal-content/DE/TXT/?uri=legissum%3Al33139
306 https://eur-lex.europa.eu/legal-content/DE/TXT/?uri=legissum%3Al14566

workers are being met. In the event of violations, corporate criminal law also applies.[307]

6.4.23.5.3 Deportations

For the return of illegal immigrants, there are common rules and procedures on return decisions, deportation, coercive measures, detention as well as procedural guarantees for affected persons and unaccompanied minors.[308] Return decisions are recognised and enforced by all Member States, irrespective of the Member State in which the person concerned is present.[309] Repatriations can be carried out from several Member States in joint flights.[310] Agreements with third countries allow for repatriation according to agreed procedures and are based on reciprocity. In principle, a state is obliged to take back its own nationals in accordance with customary international law. Agreements set out procedures for identification, re-issuance of identity cards for stateless persons, involved authorities and time limits.[311]

In the course of communitarisation, the exit procedures of the Ministry of Integration will be applied continentally and supplemented by the existing requirements if they should be stricter.[312]

6.4.23.5.4 Illegal immigration by sea

Part of international law is the principle of non-refoulement and the rescue of humans in distress at sea.[313] In the course of communitarisation, this rule is being changed, because it

---

307 Ministry of Labour - 20.7.6 Legality auditor, Ministry of Justice - 8.1.3 Corporate criminal law
308 https://eur-lex.europa.eu/legal-content/DE/TXT/?uri=legissum%3Ajl0014
309 https://eur-lex.europa.eu/legal-content/DE/TXT/?uri=legissum%3Al33154
310 https://eur-lex.europa.eu/legal-content/DE/TXT/?uri=legissum%3Al14165
311 https://eur-lex.europa.eu/legal-content/DE/TXT/?uri=legissum%3Al14163
312 Ministry of Integration - 7.9 Exit procedures
313 https://eur-lex.europa.eu/legal-content/DE/

ultimately encourages illegal immigrants to deliberately place themselves in distress at sea in order to gain admission to Continental Union territory. Illegal immigrants are informed by the coast guard that they are committing a crime punishable by 10 years detention. If they move further towards the continental coast, they are immediately remanded in custody. If illegal immigrants are in distress at sea, they are rescued by the coast guard and taken back to their port of origin. If they refuse to provide information on the port of origin, they all commit a criminal offence of attempted illegal entry, which is punished just as severely because the helpfulness of the sea rescue service has been deliberately abused.

6.4.23.5.5 Unaccompanied immigrant minors

Illegal immigrants who are minors are treated in the same way as adults. However, imprisonment does not apply to them. They are returned directly to their country of origin or turned away at the external border. Legal immigration is only open to minors who are orphans and apply for asylum at the embassy. The embassy asks the third country for corresponding death certificates.

6.4.24 Continental Union foreign policy

Continental foreign policy is concerned with uniform cooperation with all third countries. In the course of communitarisation, the foreign ministries establish the Continental Council of Foreign Ministers[314] and a Continental Foreign Office. The Continental Foreign Office takes over the support of the other ministries in multi-state negotiations outside the Continental Union, including other multinational bodies such as the G20. All member state embassies will be merged, leaving only one Continental Union embassy in a third country. Former member state embassies will be used as consulates or closed.

TXT/?uri=legissum%3A2301_3
314 Ministry of State Organisation - 8.6.3 International Council

6.4.24.1 Assistance abroad

Continental Union citizens who are abroad can get help in an emergency from the embassy or consulate of their home country. However, if that Member State has neither an embassy nor a consulate in that country, Continental Union citizens can also turn to any embassy of another Member State. There they will receive the same assistance as nationals of the country of the embassy. By means of administrative assistance from this foreign embassy to the domestic embassy, the citizen can also be assisted by his or her home country. Costs incurred can also be reimbursed after the return home if the citizen is unable to pay.[315] Those who lose their passport, have it stolen or cannot access it due to destruction or inaccessibility can obtain a returnee passport as a Continental Union citizen at any embassy of a Member State.[316]

6.4.24.2 Foreign trade

Intercontinental foreign trade, related legislation and the conclusion of international trade agreements on behalf of all member states is the exclusive responsibility of the Continental Union. It follows the rules of the World Trade Organisation (WTO)[317] . The continental customs authorities are responsible for enforcing and controlling the requirements. More details can be found in the Continental Union Customs Union.

Jointly regulated are intercontinental imports and exports, trade policy, development aid and trade defence. Goods, services, intellectual property and foreign direct investment are affected. The Continental Union's measures aim to restrict or simplify admission to and from the world market. Measures include countervailing duties on imports that are subsidised or underpriced by the country of origin. In order to enforce international trade rules, duty exemptions can be reduced,

---

315https://eur-lex.europa.eu/legal-content/DE/
TXT/?uri=legissum%3A230505_1
316https://eur-lex.europa.eu/legal-content/DE/
TXT/?uri=legissum%3Al14010b
317https://www.wto.org/

Customs can be raised, quantities of imports or exports can be restricted and state orders to affected third countries can be suspended.[318] Customs agreements with third countries and international conventions regulate the cooperation of the customs authorities of third countries with those of the Continental Union, as well as the designation, transit procedures and border controls of goods.[319]

In the course of communitarisation, the requirements and measures are only applied to the Free Market Economy. Only gradually will the other economic forms follow as soon as their requirements have been standardised. Other countries in the world are also encouraged to import several economic forms and to participate in the global division of labour in research areas.

6.4.24.3 Foreign and security policy

Continental foreign and security policy serves to ensure peace and security for the Continental Union in the world. The aim is to resolve conflicts diplomatically or democratically and to adopt punitive political measures only in the event that attempts at resolution fail. Punitive policies include the expulsion of diplomats, suspension of state visits or cooperation with the Continental Union, boycotts of cultural and sporting events, trade bans on weapons or goods that can also be used as weapons, freezing of funds, securities and real estate, visa bans and entry bans, trade bans on goods, services and technologies, and suspension of funding programmes.[320]

In the course of communitarisation, the Ministers of Foreign Affairs, in voting with each other, unanimously issue sanctions against states until the Ministry of Foreign Affairs is communitarised and a continental Minister of Foreign Affairs is directly elected. The goal during communitarisation is peace treaties with all third countries.

318https://eur-lex.europa.eu/summary/chapter/0706.html
319https://eur-lex.europa.eu/summary/chapter/1210.html
320https://eur-lex.europa.eu/legal-content/DE/
TXT/?uri=legissum%3A25_1

6.4.24.4 External relations

External relations consist of agreements with third countries. These are mostly trade agreements between all member states and third countries, but often also agreements on protective requirements for the free movement of employees, justice, security, health, environment, energy, development, science, technology, Customs and transport. Some agreements are made within the framework of international organisations, others with individual states.[321]

Part of external relations are international agreements and strategies for handling the world's oceans. In addition to the United Nations Convention on the Law of the Sea, there are agreements on the Arctic, the Atlantic, the Baltic Sea and the Mediterranean. Their aim is to protect the oceans from overfishing, excess nutrients from sewage, the input of hazardous substances, pollution and species extinction.[322]

In the course of communitarisation, the agreements are incorporated into the Law Directory and, like any other Continental Union law, can be repealed or amended by citizens. The aim of future external relations is to standardise the agreements as far as possible worldwide.

6.4.24.4.1 External relations with neighbouring continents

Regular meetings and institutions are created to strengthen external relations with neighbouring continents and to avoid conflicts. The institutions are similar to the Organization for Security and Cooperation in Europe (OSCE)[323] and the Council of Europe[324] . As soon as a member state of the Continental Union has a conflict with a neighbouring third state, mediation negotiations start. The foreign ministers of all affected states meet and look for solutions to avoid punitive political measures or even war. If there are violations of human rights and the affected states have signed an agreement on

---

321 https://eur-lex.europa.eu/summary/chapter/external_relations. html?root_default=SUM_1_CODED=28
322 https://eur-lex.europa.eu/summary/chapter/0207.html
323 https://www.osce.org/de/
324 https://www.coe.int/de/web/about-us/structure

their observance, the affected ministers meet and work out proposals for solutions or agree on punitive political measures.

6.4.25 Continental Union development aid

Continental development aid pools all the expenditure, persons and materials of the member states. It develops one country at a time instead of providing aid in several countries at the same time. It starts with the least developed regions in the developed member states of the Continental Union. Then it moves into increasingly underdeveloped regions and member states until the same standard of infrastructure for transport, health, education, economy, audit services and direct democratic participation is in place throughout the Continental Union. Then it is the turn of neighbouring third countries, and after them a neighbouring exploited continent. In addition, there is the international humanitarian aid of the United Nations, in which the Continental Union is involved. It is provided after natural disasters or during crises in affected areas.[325]

6.4.26 Continental Union enlargement

On the policy agenda of the Ministry of Foreign Affairs is not only the communitarisation of the existing member states of the Continental Union, but also the enlargement of the Continental Union. The enlargement finds its limits in the continental expansion of the continent. All states that are not member states in the Continental Union but lie within the continental expansion area are considered candidates for accession. Candidate countries adapt their political structures, processes and contents to the uniform standard of the other member states in the outer ring before they join. The adaptation is accompanied by the Continental Union institution and supports candidate countries in the introduction of existing Continental Union law.

---

[325] https://eur-lex.europa.eu/summary/chapter/1107.html

6.5 United States of the Continent[326]

The unified states of the continent are the goal to be achieved in the inner ring of the Continental Union. Even if there are initially several federal states in the inner ring of the Continental Union, they are to unify in the future. For unification between federal states, the three rings of integration are again run-through. For example, there could be two federal states in the north and south, which only later unite to form the United States of the Continents. All member states of the Continental Union that cannot join the unified states of the continent because the people reject it in voting remain in the middle or outer ring of the Continental Union.

The conditions for uniform living standards are created by continental trade in four different economic forms. The uniform law and state organisational conditions are created by the communitarisation of the ministries in the outer and middle rings. The national borders are shared by the member states, with exclaves allowed if they are on the same continent. For example, different states can form a federal state, although one of the participants does not share an external border with the other states. The deciding factor is that they share the Continental Union's common continental external border. The federal state that this country joins must have a constitution that guarantees the citizens at least the same rights as the constitution of the dynamic media democracy.

6.5.1 Continental Constitution

The constitutional process of the continental constitution takes place primarily between the member states that wish to establish a federal state with each other. Secondarily, the other member states of the Continental Union are also involved. Their politicians are to give opinions on the constitutional articles. The citizens of the other member states can also vote on the constitution, while the citizens of the desired federal state vote on it. The votes of the citizens in the other member states are used for statistical purposes. This is to provide a

---

326 §168.2 World peace

picture of opinion on how likely constitutional changes will be in future accessions.

The constitution of the unified states of the continent shall be direct democratic and federal in character, similar to the constitution for the dynamic media democracy. The constitution may be amended by the people at any time and by candidate countries after approval by the peoples involved.[327] To this end, each article is put to a vote individually and those articles that fall below 90% approval are newly formulated in constitutional committees .[328]

6.5.2 Cultural integration[329]

Cultural integration is slower than political integration. Therefore, the unified states of the continent continue to pursue a culture integration policy.

In the unified states of the continent, a common language is spoken and taught as the first foreign language from primary school onwards. Whether this should be a new or spoken language is decided by the citizens in a referendum. If it is to be a new language, it is decided on committees together with the citizens. Words and grammatical rules can be contributed by the individual peoples.[330]

The leading cultural religion in continental legal history is taken into account. State and religion are separated. Religious institutions offering goods or services unrelated to religious practice are prohibited. The state makes regulations for religions on how religion may be practised in the country. Exceptions apply in various regions.[331]

For example, certain municipalities may decide against wearing the veil in public and banning minarets. In some localities, Muslims are not allowed to live or work or stay longer than for transit. In an opposite example, certain regions may join municipalities to be Muslim. Women everywhere must be veiled and the muezzin calls for prayer five times a day. The

327 Ministry of State Organisation - 9.11 Constitutional Amendments
328 Ministry of State Organisation - 9.11.2 Constitutional Committee
329 §185,3 Languages
330 Ministry of Integration - 6.1 Official languages
331 Ministry of Integration - 6.3 Cultural protection area

Social Market Economy there may include Muslim economic commandments. In some localities, people of other faiths are banned except for transit, and Sharia police patrol the area and may collect a monetary fine for indecent dress or sentence former partners to Non-profit work in cases of adultery.

The sentences are limited to expulsions for transients. For residents, sentences must not involve the use of force or deprivation of liberty and must be in accordance with the constitution. All articles of the constitution and the same penal laws apply everywhere in the unified states of the continent, influenced by popular votes and the religious values in the population as a whole. In the course of worldwide communitarisation, the imprints of world religions in national laws merge into international laws. Citizens decide in constitutional committees[332] , which religious values they consider so valuable that all humans on earth should adhere to them.

7 International policy

The Ministry of Foreign Affairs is responsible for participating in international policy. It can take its own initiatives or act on orders from ministries. It is guided by the principle of international order, consisting of international organisations and intergovernmental treaties in an environment of global anarchy, where the law of the strongest still applies. The aim of the international policy of the Ministry of Foreign Affairs is to transform global anarchy into a global dynamic media democracy through communitarisation. The law of the strongest is replaced by democratically negotiated laws.

The first approach is to create an international code that brings together all previous internationally identical rules and can be increasingly expanded through communitarisation. It becomes part of the Law Directory, giving all its rules a repeal quorum. If such a quorum is triggered, the validity of the international rule is negotiated inland in a committee. In the negotiations, an alternative proposal must be developed and put to a vote of the people. If the alternative proposal is approved, the foreign minister is thereby given the orders to

332 Ministry of State Organisation - 9.11.2 Constitutional Committee

newly negotiate with the member states or to withdraw from the agreement.

The Ministry of Foreign Affairs maintains intergovernmental relations with as many countries as possible through its embassies around the world. It also maintains a representation at the United Nations[333] , which is responsible for elections, candidacies and documentation of United Nations bodies. The representative assumes voting rights for elections, votes, resolutions and speeches, in voting with the foreign minister. Candidacies of domestic politicians at the United Nations are prepared in voting with the affected parties. The Minister of Foreign Affairs, in voting with the Minister of Security, may deploy parts of the military as United Nations blue helmet soldiers for peacekeeping missions.

7.1 International institutions

International policy takes place predominantly in international organisations and intergovernmental partnerships. It encompasses all policy areas and is partly communitarised by similar laws and standards. A rule of law or a monopoly on the use of force, on the other hand, is hardly developed. International laws are given, for example, by international law and are used, for example, by the International Court of Justice[334] to justify judgements. Independent jurisdictions, So-called International Arbitration Courts,[335] are usually created for economic treaties between states.

The Ministry of Foreign Affairs represents the country at meetings of heads of state and government. All supranational and intergovernmental bodies outside the Continental Union are shifted to the United Nations as soon as possible. So-called summits of rich countries, So-called industrialised nations, such as G7, G8 and G20, serve as opportunities for intergovernmental treaties and voting on attitudes to international communitarisation. In the course of

---

333https://www.un.org/en/
334https://www.icc-cpi.int/
335https://www.international-arbitration-attorney.com/de/international-court-of-arbitration/

communitarisation, such negotiations are held in public and concluded in a direct democratic manner. This is to avoid industrialised nations forming an alliance that is able to exploit poorer or underdeveloped countries with their multinational corporations. The creation of jobs does not outweigh the profits flowing abroad. But if the profits remain in the underdeveloped countries, they strengthen the purchasing power there and the peoples can catch up more quickly with their standard of living.

7.2 International law[336]

The Ministry of Foreign Affairs is responsible for approving international treaties, international law and existing international law. Regardless of which ministry is affected, the Minister of Foreign Affairs is responsible for overseeing the intergovernmental negotiation and voting by the people on the negotiated treaty.

Municipalities can be declared responsible through a subsidiarity vote, a municipal law or a treaty under international law. In this case, either the municipal foreign minister or the deputy foreign ministers of the municipalities affected are responsible for approving international law treaties.

International law does not apply directly, but must be converted into laws in the states. In contrast to natural law, it is not natural laws that apply, but laws enacted by humans in states that apply within national borders. International law, in the broadest sense, has been set by humanity. It is to be seen as the first step towards a worldwide communitarisation. Whereas in the past it came into being within the framework of a meeting of heads of state, in future it is to be created in international organisations with the democratic participation of the affected citizens.

Existing international law can be amended or repealed by

336§167 Implementation of international law treaties: BV Art. 141a, §166.2 Relations with foreign countries and treaties under international law: BV Art.166. Dolzer, Rudolf: International law, in: Nohlen, Dieter; Schultze, Rainer-Olaf (eds.) 2004: Lexikon der Politikwissenschaft. Theorien, Methoden, Begriffe, C.H.Beck, Munich, pp.1072-1075, ISBN 3406511279.

the people after a repeal quorum has been triggered in the Law Directory.[337] This gives the foreign minister the order to withdraw approval and, if necessary, to ask the community of states to negotiate a new treaty or just individual sections. By including international law in the Law Directory, citizens can decide which parts of international law and which formulations should be changed or whether their country should withdraw from the agreed treaty under international law. International law currently enables an inter-state coordination order because it only applies to states. It only acquires a policy steering function for citizens when it is democratised.

7.2.1 Democratisation of international law

International law is currently undemocratic because the separation of powers is abolished even for democratic states. Heads of government and their ministers belong to the executive, i.e. the executive power. However, through the statutes of international law, they fulfil the task of the legislative power, the legislation. If then, in international law, intergovernmental Arbitration Courts and international tribunals without communitarisation of the Ministry of Justice dispense justice, the executive also has the judicial power of the judiciary. An international organisation whose members also consist of the executive assumes the moderation between the negotiating partners and thus the mediating power of the mediative.

In the course of communitarisation, the powers are also shared internationally, the persons primarily responsible become directly elected politicians of their ministry or agency.[338] International law becomes uniform laws that apply in all member states and can be influenced at any time via the repeal quorum.[339]

---

337 Ministry of Justice - 4.7 Law Directory, Ministry of State Organisation - 9.5.15 Repeal quorum
338 Ministry of State Organisation - 7 Separation of powers
339 Ministry of State Organisation - 9.5.15 Repeal quorum

7.2.2 Mandatory provisions of international law[340]

When amending the constitution, the mandatory provisions of international law must not be violated. Mandatory provisions of international law are the requirement of non-violence, the protection of the environment for descendants and the granting of human rights.

Non-violence is explained in international law for peace and war. International law of peace regulates when the use of military force is lawful. International law of war, also called international humanitarian law, regulates lawful action in war. Diplomacy is used instead of force. The Vienna Convention on Diplomatic Relations, which was customary law until 1961, is also considered international law.[341] It regulates diplomatic relations between states. In the course of the communitarisation of the united states of the world, diplomatic relations are replaced by democratic relations between states in an International Union.

In order to protect the environment and guarantee human rights, decisions are made on the basis of general legal principles. General principles of law are that treaties must be respected, the more specific law must prevail over the more general law, the later law must prevail over a previous one, and good faith must prevail in the absence of contradictions between the past and the future. The protection of the environment is achieved by transferring the environment to humanity and by humanity becoming a subject of international law. As a subject of international law, humanity can then also assert human rights internationally as rights to which it is directly entitled. International environmental law concerns the law of the sea, air and space law, as well as international law aspects of the Arctic Ocean, the Antarctic and international watercourses. In the course of the communitarisation of the ministries of labour, infrastructure and health, uniform standards for the protection of the environment are created. Authorities of these ministries audit compliance with the standards and impose bans or sentences for non-compliance. States and persons

---

340 §257.8 Constitutional initiative: BV Art. 139
341 https://legal.un.org/ilc/texts/instruments/english/conventions/9_1_1961.pdf

who violate environmental protection regulations are brought before the international criminal court and, if convicted, are subject to United Nations sanctions. In the medium term, the locally responsible United States of the Continents supervise their air, land and sea areas. In the long term, only the united states of the world will be responsible. Space law is never communitarised between the United States of the Continents, but always between all states.

Human rights, which were laid down by the United Nations General Assembly in a resolution in 1948,[342] form the basis for rights granted to all humans under their constitutions. Human rights are considered communitarised as soon as they are enshrined in the constitutions of the member states. At the same time, human rights mark the beginning of the formulation of a constitution for the united states of the world.

7.2.3 Customary international law

Customary international law arises when all participants behave in the same way because they assume such a principle of conduct. This can give rise to customary international law if, for example, a state adheres to the principles of an international treaty without having signed it. In principle, customary international law can be replaced or superseded by democratically created laws. This is linked to the principle that each generation may make its own rules as long as they do not burden future generations. Deceased generations should not be allowed to impose constraints on living and future generations, except the constraint not to burden future generations. Any law, be it customary international law or national law, can be changed by humans at any time through democratic negotiation and majority voting.

342https://www.un.org/depts/german/menschenrechte/aemr.pdf

7.2.4 Supranational law

Supranational law also counts as international law because it is located above the states. An International Union provides supranational law through communitarisation in the outer and middle ring through common laws and ministries. In this way, part of the sovereign power of several member states is surrendered. An example of this is the Continental Union with its regulations. This contrasts with international law, which is agreed upon by international organisations on an intergovernmental basis. The sovereign power remains with the states. They agree on the same laws or standards by treaty. An example of this is the United Nations with its resolutions.

7.2.5 Private international law

Private international law does not count as international law because states determine in their ministries how they deal with foreigners. For example, the Ministry of Integration sets the quota of foreigners for its country in voting with the people. Other states are not involved in the decision. In the case of treaties within an International Union, on the other hand, all the involved peoples must vote on the treaty before it can come into force.

7.2.6 Subjects of international law

States and international organisations that can create international law are considered subjects of international law. In principle, peoples can jointly create international law. International non-governmental organisations (NGOs) and multinational companies or persons are not considered subjects of international law, even if they operate across borders and conclude treaties to this end. Such agreements only become international law when states or ministries decide to introduce them as identical laws in all participating states.

7.2.7 International criminal law

In contrast to conventional international law, international criminal law applies not only to states, but also to individuals who, in the course of their state activities, commit crimes that also affect other states or violate human rights. This refers to genocide, crimes against humanity, war crimes and crimes of aggression, i.e. wars of aggression. The International Criminal Court is responsible for international criminal law. In the course of communitarisation, the International Criminal Court becomes responsible for human rights violations and violations of international environmental law until it ends up as a Remit Court of the Ministry of Justice.

The Ministry of Foreign Affairs, with the help of its embassies, ensures the registration of criminals subject to international criminal law and their arrest by the security agencies inland. The arrested persons are transferred to the International Criminal Court. From the communitarisation of international criminal law and the International Criminal Court, the Ministry of Justice takes over court proceedings and detentions.

7.2.8 International disputes[343]

In the event of international disputes, the Ministry of Foreign Affairs ensures that conflicts between states and municipalities are discussed and solutions negotiated. International disputes can be resolved either through diplomatic, democratic or judicial procedures. How disputes are to be resolved is already laid down in inter-state treaties or international law. Diplomatic procedures consist of newly conducted negotiations between the parties to a treaty, investigations by a United Nations committee and mediation with the participation of a Negotiator to reach a compromise. Judicial proceedings are held before the International Court of Justice[344] when states accuse each other of violations of United Nations international law. When citizens or companies of different states accuse each other of breaching an international

343§168,1,7 World peace: BV Art. 173
344https://www.icj-cij.org/en

treaty, they resort to interstate Arbitration Courts[345] . If a state has committed an alleged offence under international criminal law, the International Criminal Court[346] is called in.

In the course of communitarisation, the current procedures are democratised. Negotiations then take place between directly elected ministers or an international council.[347] Enquiries are conducted in a committee of enquiry,[348] and mediations are held by the Federal Moderator or in a committee.[349]

In international judicial proceedings, the plaintiffs and defendants must have the possibility to lodge an appeal and a revision.[350] The final instance is then not the National Court of Justice, but the International Court of Justice. All other courts for political contents, such as the International Tribunal for the Law of the Sea[351] , are run as chambers in the international court. Interstate Arbitration Courts must either be housed in Chambers of a Court of the International Union of its Member States or in the International Court of Justice.

7.2.9 United Nations

The international organisation of the United Nations[352] is an intergovernmental association of 193 nations. Each state has one vote and all states have equal rights. In the Security Council, however, only five permanent members still have a veto.

In the course of communitarisation, it is transformed into an International Union. Member states can then adopt common laws and communitarise ministries.

---

345 https://www.international-arbitration-attorney.com/de/international-court-of-arbitration/
346 https://www.icc-cpi.int/
347 Ministry of State Organisation - 8.3.1 Minister, 8.6.3 International Council
348 Ministry of State Organisation - 12.5.2 Committee of enquiry, 12.5 Punitive measures for politicians
349 Ministry of State Organisation - 4.4 Federal Moderator's Office, 9.6 Committee
350 Ministry of Justice - 5.1 Legal process
351 https://www.itlos.org/en/
352 https://www.un.org/en/

7.2.9.1 Charter of the United Nations

The Charter of the United Nations[353] is considered the constitution on the basis of which the international organisation acts. The United Nations Charter lays down the general prohibition of the use of force, according to which states may not wage a war of aggression. The only exception is the right of self-defence. The United Nations Charter sets out the objectives of international peace, respect for international law and human rights, and intergovernmental cooperation, and how they are to be pursued.

In the course of communitarisation, the contents of the United Nations Charter are incorporated into the constitution of the united states of the world.

7.2.9.2 General Assembly

All member states are assembled in the General Assembly. It decides on the budget and can discuss all international issues that are not also dealt with in the Security Council. So-called resolutions are drafted and voted on in order to issue recommendations for action to the member states. Resolutions are not international law and do not have to be converted into national law. The General Assembly can best be seen as an international council of foreign ministers. Thematic work, which is subdivided by remit, is done in committees and working groups.

7.2.9.3 International Law Commission

The International Law Commission ensures the formulation and codification of customary international law into set law, which states can agree to and thereby accede to. In the course of communitarisation, the International Law Commission becomes responsible for assigning existing international law to the ministries' areas of accountability.

---

353 https://www.un.org/en/about-us/un-charter

7.2.9.4 International Court of Justice

Only states have admission to the international court[354] , not international organisations or citizens. It is only responsible if the states have signed a declaration of submission or if international law treaties stipulate its responsibility, which the states involved confirm by their signature.

7.2.9.5 Security Council

The United Nations Security Council has 15 member states, 5 of which are permanent members and the only states with a veto. Resolutions can be passed there that become binding because the Security Council has a monopoly on the use of force with which it can enforce coercive measures. It can decide on sanctions and enforce them with coercive measures if necessary. Its composition and procedure are undemocratic, but capable of preventing world wars. In the course of communitarisation, all member states become permanent members and pass resolutions with a majority of 90%. Resolutions that result in warlike actions or the use of force are voted on by the peoples. Once all the states of the world communitarise their security ministries, it is fully democratised.

7.2.9.6 United Nations sanctions

Sanctions are sentences that do not take effect through military force, but through isolation. This includes the interruption of economic relations, transport and communication routes as well as the severance of diplomatic relations.

7.2.10 Arms control[355]

The Ministry of Foreign Affairs shall ensure arms control in voting with the ministries of security and labour and with other states and their ministries of security and labour or economy. It is constitutionally prohibited to export weapons of war

---

354https://www.icj-cij.org/en
355§225.5 Foreign economic policy

abroad.[356] In addition, the people can restrict or prohibit the export of weapons abroad for a limited or unlimited period by a quorum of 40%. Compliance with national and international requirements is monitored by the Company Auditing Agency and Customs.[357]

The Ministry of Foreign Affairs is involved in the international treaties, summits and control measures for nuclear, chemical, biological and conventional disarmament. The Non-Proliferation Treaty (NPT)[358] regulates the disarmament of all nuclear weapons and the peaceful use of nuclear energy and is monitored by the International Atomic Energy Agency (IAEA)[359] . The Nuclear Suppliers Group (NSG)[360] checks companies and goods supplies to see whether they contribute to the proliferation of nuclear weapons. To protect against nuclear terrorism, control measures on the worldwide proliferation of nuclear explosive material have emerged from the Nuclear Security Summit (NSS)[361] . The Ministry of Foreign Affairs is striving for the same efforts for biological and chemical agents.

For conventional weapons of war, the Organization for Security and Cooperation in Europe (OSCE) operates[362] confidence- and security-building measures (CSBMs)[363] . The treaty on conventional armed forces in Europe[364] agrees on numerical ceilings for military vehicles and aircraft. With the Vienna Document[365] , the agreement to send and receive observers and military personnel for the exchange of information applies. During their visits, they control the movement, stationing and number of military devices on land, at sea and in the air in the States Parties. With the Open Skies Treaty[366] ,

---

356 §225,5,6 Foreign trade policy, §223,2 Weapons and war material: BV Art. 107

357 Ministry of Labour - 20 Company Auditing Agency, Ministry of Security - 8 Customs

358 https://www.un.org/disarmament/wmd/nuclear/npt/

359 https://www.iaea.org/

360 https://www.nuclearsuppliersgroup.org/en/about-nsg

361 https://www.gusp.org/news/2016_04_03_forbes/

362 https://www.osce.org

363 https://www.osce.org/arms-control

364 https://www.osce.org/library/14087

365 https://www.osce.org/fsc/86597

366 https://www.osce.org/library/14127

overflights with aerial photographs are agreed for arms control in all States Parties. The Ministry of Foreign Affairs advocates such confidence- and security-building measures at the global level in the United Nations. The first step in this direction is the Missile Technology Control Regime (MTCR)[367] , which prevents the proliferation of missiles, cruise missiles and drones capable of carrying nuclear, biological or chemical weapons. The control regime provides for the enactment of laws on export controls for missile technology in the States Parties and the monitoring of compliance with these laws. Similar export controls are established by the Wassenaar Agreement[368] for conventional weapons and military and civilian goods and technologies. In order to ensure arms control in trade between the signatory states, standards are set for pre-shipment inspection. The Ministry of Foreign Affairs is committed to ensuring that no State Party supplies goods or means of production for military use to a war zone or to dictatorships.

In the course of communitarisation, arms control is being expanded so that fewer and fewer armaments are necessary and permissible. As more and more peace treaties are concluded and states are united in confederations, less military is needed. In the united states of the world, there are only military defences against threats from outer space. Only such armaments will then still be permissible. Confidence- and security-building measures can continue to exist.

7.3 International policy areas

The Ministry of Foreign Affairs, together with the Foreign Office, its embassies and representations, coordinates international policy areas with the responsible domestic and international ministries. Ministers can submit topics to the Foreign Office that are to be internationally unified or communitarised.

The Ministry of Foreign Affairs ensures global networking so that the most effective policy and economic measures are

367 https://mtcr.info/
368 https://www.wassenaar.org/

identified and shared with all member states.[369]

7.3.1 International politics of state organisation

The Ministry of State Organisation provides for international responsibilities in federalism, global policy, the international council and international party council in state and administrative law.[370] The external borders and institutions for communitarisation are voted on jointly by the affected peoples.[371]   Otherwise,   international   organisations, intergovernmental diplomatic relations and international unions are considered political structures and processes at the international level.

7.3.2 International security and justice policy

An international police force exists only in some states that involve their police forces in Interpol[372]. One could call the United Nations blue helmet soldiers[373] an international army, which depends on the military of the member states. In terms of its composition of member states and majority ratios, the United Nations Security Council is the beginning of an international council for security ministries. In the course of communitarisation, peace treaties are concluded, armies are merged and finally dismantled. In order to avoid a world war by then, a global defence alliance is founded, in which NATO is merged and at least all nuclear powers are members. The police forces, customs investigators and Tax Investigation Departments initially exchange their data to fight crime. As soon as the Ministry of Security is communitarised in the middle ring, the security agencies work across borders. In

---

369 Ministry of Labour - 20.7.3.5.11.1 Certification of Success Models, 20.9 Success Model Directory
370 Ministry of State Organisation - 11.3 Responsibilities in federalism, 11.4 Global policy, 8.6.3 International Council, 8.6.4.3 International Party Council
371 Ministry of State Organisation - 9.7.5.1 Peoples
372 https://www.interpol.int/
373 https://www.un.org/en/our-work/maintain-international-peace-and-security

the case of different legal situations by ministries that have not yet been communitarised, the offender must be brought before a court in the member state where he is alleged to have committed the crime. Once the Ministry of Justice is communitarised, the place of jurisdiction is irrelevant. For all cases involving international law, the international court becomes ultimately responsible.

The Ministry of Labour is responsible for auditing foreign trade crimes of corruption, money laundering, financing of terrorism, mafia organisations, negative externalities and cybercrime through the Company Auditing Agency and reporting the cases to the police and the Foreign Office.[374]

7.3.3 International infrastructure policy

The Ministry of Infrastructure pursues the international infrastructure policy of self-sufficiency and specialisation as well as the rapid transport of goods and persons. According to this policy, all states should be able to meet the basic needs of their populations for energy and raw materials on their own. Depending on the natural regional conditions, specialisation in the production of energy and raw materials as well as in the means of transport are envisaged. In order to facilitate rapid transport, the networks will be expanded as uniformly as possible and equipped with the fastest and most environmentally friendly means of transport.

7.3.3.1 International transport policy[375]

The Ministry of Foreign Affairs takes over the negotiations for cross-border traffic and coordinates its approach with the Ministry of Infrastructure. The International Civil Aviation Organisation (ICAO)[376] regulates the standards for aircraft and overflight rights in international aviation law. Only aircraft that comply with the standards are allowed to use

---

374 Ministry of Labour - 20.7.6 Legality auditors, Ministry of Security - 7 Police
375 Ministry of Infrastructure - 8 Traffic
376 https://www.icao.int/Pages/default.aspx

domestic airspace. Companies and states are granted overflight rights if they do not pose a threat to the environment or the population. If the situation changes, overflight rights can be withdrawn for a limited period on the instructions of the foreign minister. The same applies to foreign ships wishing to use domestic waters and foreign vehicles wishing to use domestic roads or railways. In voting with the Ministry of Infrastructure, a fee may be charged for the use of domestic transport infrastructure for foreigners.

In the course of communitarisation, transport routes and means of transport are being adapted to each other worldwide to enable borderless, low-noise and pollution-free movement. The states are increasingly adapting their standards to each other for this purpose. In the medium term, magnetic levitation technology will transport persons and goods by rail over land and underground on long-distance intercontinental routes.

7.3.3.2 Foreign energy policy

In the course of communitarisation, cross-border energy interconnections are being set up. This is intended to bridge regional temporary outages. The states agree on a uniform voltage grid so that all electrical devices can be used worldwide without an adapter.

The Ministry of Foreign Affairs works within the community of states towards a global energy supply through renewable energies. In the course of communitarisation, a global energy interconnection network is being established, based on two pillars. First, future buildings will be able to support themselves with sufficient energy from their surroundings. Secondly, the industrial use of energy is made possible through power plants for water, wind and sun. These power plants are available in all regions and are able to support their region with sufficient energy on their own. In parts of the world that are particularly well suited to a particular renewable energy source, power plants can be operated more economically than elsewhere. Normally, these regions generate the energy for all of humanity. But if there are failures or shortages, the regional power plants are switched on. This oversupply of energy can reduce costs and ensure security of supply despite rising energy consumption.

After the switch to renewable energy and energy storage, surplus energy can be supplied to foreign countries. The global energy transition from finite to renewable energy sources will be accomplished in the short term by using less energy from coal, oil and natural gas and more nuclear power until sufficient capacity is provided by renewables. The principle applies that it is better to store nuclear waste safely than to pollute the air and groundwater, which means incalculable damage and follow-up costs for an incalculably long time.

The construction of nuclear power plants should be avoided because the costs are better invested in renewable energies. Even if the construction costs seem to be cheaper in the short term with nuclear power and coal-fired power, there are incalculably long and high costs for disposal for future generations. Mines for coal mining are backfilled and sealed to avoid poisoning global water reserves with mine water.[377]

Biomass and bioenergy from agriculture land is the last to go abroad after domestic demand has been met.[378] Biomass that is supplied as waste from abroad because there are not yet any plants for recycling is imported until the capacities are utilised. 30% of the resulting profits are invested in the procurement of a recycling plant. As soon as the necessary amount is reached, the recycling plant is delivered to the affected foreigner. In the course of communitarisation, biomass is integrated into the global circular economy by being filtered and recycled by wastewater treatment plants and recycling centres before being released into the environment. The resulting end products, such as fertiliser, gas, heat and electricity, are considered energy, as it were.

---

377 Ministry of Infrastructure - 9.5 Energy transition
378 Ministry of Infrastructure - 4.3.2 Agricultural land

7.3.3.3 Foreign raw materials policy

External commodity policy involves the import of commodities that are scarce or unavailable domestically and the export of available commodities whose domestic demand is met. The import of raw materials is given a price premium that encourages the development of substitutes. In the course of communitarisation, a global circular economy is developed that does not require finite raw materials.[379] In order to avoid international exploitation, the same prices for raw materials apply worldwide as far as possible. The price may then only be adjusted to natural circumstances. For example, bamboo can build up more biomass much faster in parts of the world, which is why the price for this raw material can be cheaper in the affected countries. In the course of communitarisation, all renewable raw materials are cultivated in the most favourable places worldwide.

7.3.3.4 International waste disposal

The export of waste abroad is prohibited. The import of waste is only permitted if it can be disposed of without residues and in an environmentally neutral manner or if it is completely recyclable. The Ministry of Foreign Affairs, in cooperation with the Ministry of Infrastructure, promotes the marketing of advanced waste disposal technology.[380] In cooperation with the ministries of economy, production and packaging are adapted to current disposal possibilities. As a general rule, nothing may be produced or imported that cannot be disposed of.

The Ministry of Foreign Affairs is seeking funding and joint implementation of international waste management in the international community. This affects the oceans polluted with plastic and the Earth's orbit interspersed with space debris. The Ministry of Infrastructure develops and markets suitable mobile disposal facilities in cooperation with the Ministry of Innovation.

379 Ministry of Infrastructure - 4.3 Natural Resources, 4.9.2 Waste disposal
380 Ministry of Infrastructure - 4.9.2 Waste disposal

The further spreading of space debris should be made a worldwide sentence. Deliberately endangering the Earth by making it a prison because its orbit is riddled with billions of small projectiles is considered deliberate killing of future generations. Operators of devices in Earth orbit will be required to pay for the research and implementation of the disposal of their space debris.[381]

7.3.3.5 International water supply

Domestic water supply must be guaranteed before it can be used abroad. Limits and rights of use are set by the Ministry of Infrastructure for domestic companies. Rights and standards for the use of international watercourses are set in cooperation with the Ministry of Foreign Affairs. A policy of decreasing water pollution is pursued, ending with waters that are drinkable worldwide. Even if the oceans with their saltwater are not among these waters, they are still to be kept free of human waste. The protection requirements are directed at ships and aircraft as well as at wastewater treatment plants in front of river mouths on coasts. The Ministry of Foreign Affairs ensures the marketing of river treatment plants that are capable of cleaning entire rivers.[382]

The comprehensive global water supply with drinking, fresh and waste water is provided by the infrastructure ministries of the community of states through pipelines, wells and desalination plants in the course of communitarisation.

7.3.4 International integration policy

With communitarisation, the Ministry of Foreign Affairs works towards breaking down borders between states by unifying political structures, processes and contents. In voting with the Ministry of Integration, care is taken to ensure that the political contents of policies on foreigners, culture and religion are so detached from the other political contents that

381 Ministry of Infrastructure - 8.10.2.1 Space debris
382 Ministry of Infrastructure - 4.9.1 Water supply, 4.9.2.2 Waste treatment plants

they do not hold back communitarisation. This is to allow for two different speeds of integration, one for constitutions and laws, and another for cultural manners and customs. Experience shows that it takes longer for humans to get used to new cultural manners and customs than to a new political system. With its international integration policy, the Ministry of Integration ensures that the political system can be communitarised worldwide more quickly than cultural manners and customs. Through a world language, all humans are to speak at least one common language in the future, in order to enable the integration or assimilation of humans.

7.3.4.1 Policy on foreigners

quota of foreigners[383] are used to manage the rate of immigration and to decide whether integration or assimilation is desired. Two different quotas of foreign nationals for similar or dissimilar cultural groups take into account the different integration effort. While the quotas of foreign nationals are lower for foreigners from the same International Union because there is greater cultural similarity, they are higher for foreigners from third countries.

In a globalised world, immigration should happen out of love for the country and its people, not out of need and poverty. Therefore, foreigners who permanently reside in another country are exempt from punishment and payment.[384] The community of states ensures appropriate repatriation agreements.[385]

In the course of communitarisation, the quotas of foreign nationals in the inner ring cease to apply to nationals of member states because they are now nationals of a new federal state.

---

383 Ministry of Integration - 7.4 Quota of foreigners
384 Ministry of Integration - 7.5 Immigration conditions
385 Ministry of Integration - 7.9 Exit procedures

7.3.4.2 Religious policy

The community of states intervenes in religious freedom to enable world peace. The freedom of faith of the individual is not interfered with. All world religions should name their commonalities in order to reconcile the believers with each other. Religions that want to continue to divide the world population in order to discriminate against one part may only be practised in cultural protection areas[386] . State and church are separated in the course of communitarisation.[387]

7.3.4.3 Cultural policy

In the world society, the borders between humans should disappear, not necessarily culturally, but financially and politically. This will result in fewer countries, which can then move towards each other to grow together into a world society. In the world society there will then be different languages, manners and customs. There will be cosmopolitan cities, municipalities or unifications of municipalities with a global mixed culture, but also regions that want to separate themselves culturally. The ministries, through a federal and subsidiary organisation, will ensure that the citizens of the united states of the world enjoy this freedom and that their survival as a people is assured.[388]

Developing into a world society and, in the process, harmonising the manners and customs that are rich in generations is the goal of the state's integration measures.[389] Manners and customs that do not fit together should not be banned or abolished, but should be allowed in cultural protection areas, provided there are enough humans who want to care for them. The constitution applies everywhere, but locally exceptions or additions to laws are possible and must be pointed out at the entrance to the village. Freedom of movement remains guaranteed. Settlement, on the other

---

386 Ministry of Integration - 6.3 Cultural protection area
387 Ministry of Integration - 6.4 Religious communities, 6.5 Religion management
388 Ministry of State Organisation - 10 Subsidiarity, 11 Federalism
389 Ministry of Integration - 7.7 Integration measures

hand, as a tourist, resident, trader, employee, entrepreneur or visitor can be restricted, but not transit.[390]
The aim should be that cultures and races of humanity can survive in cultural protection areas. Cultures can be handed down if necessary, i.e. they can be stored in the media. The diversity of the races of the human species in particular must be preserved. It is crucial to keep the human races close to the genetic material of the species, so that a shielded race does not develop into a separate species at some point, i.e. these humans are no longer able to produce fertile offspring with other humans outside the cultural protection area. Racial diversity should make it possible to maintain resistance in the human genome to pathogens or evolutionary adaptation to natural conditions. If necessary, this genetic material can be introduced into the rest of the human gene pool as soon as natural circumstances change or epidemics rage.

7.3.4.4 World language[391]

In the United Nations, the Ministry of Foreign Affairs is trying to make sign language a world language. Speaking at the same time becomes possible because humans can speak in their own language and also use their arms and hands. Children learn much faster because they are able to express themselves earlier through gestures.
Braille is to be used as the script. Written characters are more difficult to learn and draw than the arrangement of dots.
A new language is invented as a spoken and grammatical language. One word or grammatical peculiarity from each language of the world flows into the new language. Which word or grammar this should be is decided by all the humans who speak this language. When choosing, care should be taken to use a word or grammar that is culturally typical of the people or peoples where the language is considered the national language. All other words are new and should be easy to learn, speak and understand.

---

390 Ministry of State Organisation - 11.5.7 Cultural protection areas for the protection of minorities
391 §185,3 Languages

An existing language must not become the world language, as is currently the case with English. In this way, only one people would be favoured and given the right to spread their culture of life, because language is the highest cultural asset of humanity, because every human expresses himself to other humans with it.

7.3.5 International digital policy

The Ministry of Digital Affairs ensures the worldwide distribution of the intranet through open source programmes and operating systems. This enables each state to carry out the digital transformation of state management on its own authority. As soon as the ministries for media and digital are communitarised, citizens can also be digitally involved in international decision-making.[392] Until then, the laws of a state apply to its intranet.

The internet remains alongside the state-controlled intranet. The respective states are responsible for their intranet, whereas the international community is responsible for the internet. In the transition phase, necessary applications will be moved from the intranet to areas of the internet that are as secure as possible so that as many peoples as possible can participate.

In the course of communitarisation, general rules for security on the internet are negotiated. This includes international criminal legislation for the internet and prosecution by international police authorities.

7.3.6 International media policy

The Ministry of Media Affairs sends foreign correspondents to report from abroad for state television. They work with the embassy and consulates or representations in the affected countries. They may occupy common premises to save costs or provide increased security.

The Ministry of Foreign Affairs ensures the international

392Ministry of Digital Affairs - 9 Digital Economy, 11.3 Admission, 15.5.9 Game Variations

cooperation of the state media institutions and the borderless dissemination possibility also for private press and media products, such as newspapers or films. Foreign correspondents can work and broadcast in the newsrooms of state media broadcasters from member states. State broadcasters from member states are increasingly producing joint shows, documentaries and feature films.

Worldwide freedom of the press, with orders for journalists to report objectively, is the goal of the Ministry of Foreign Affairs' negotiations with other states or international organisations.

In the course of the communitarisation of the Ministry of Media Affairs, freedom of information is implemented in all states. Censorship is now only applied in the case of criminal offences, which includes knowingly false reporting.

The News Television provides translation and summaries of international news programmes. The Government Television provides an international participation opportunity with its show on consultations by translating the show into the national languages of the member states and making it available worldwide via the internet.[393] The final voting on the international treaty takes place at the voting computers in the polling stations.

In the course of communitarisation, the broadcasting area in the outer ring of the International Union is extended to all member states. In the middle ring, the search area and field of action are extended to all member states.

7.3.7 International innovation policy

The Ministry of Foreign Affairs promotes international cooperation in science and research in voting with the Ministries of Innovation and Education.

Science and innovation houses[394] are used to network joint state or private and corporate research and development activities. They also fulfil the task of bringing innovations from around the world more quickly to the domestic market.

393 Ministry of Media Affairs - 8.1 Programme, 7.2.3.7 Consultations
394 https://www.auswaertiges-amt.de/de/aussenpolitik/themen/kulturdialog/-/213142

Conversely, they promote domestic People's Innovation Company innovations and products through exhibitions and sales events. They regularly inform the innovation auditors and the Innovation Agency[395] about innovations abroad.

In order to be able to market innovations more quickly in companies and to make it easier for consumers to switch, international standardisation and product standards are being developed. In addition, all countries are pooling their databases for industrial property rights to make it easier to search for innovations.[396] The Ministry of Foreign Affairs, in voting with the Ministry of Innovation, is working for the rapid communitarisation of patent offices so that it will be possible to apply for a worldwide patent easily and quickly. In the course of communitarisation, the regions of the world specialise in different areas of research and development.[397] Citizens can vote together on research projects.[398] If a research project then moves forward quickly because the majority of citizens agree and approve the corresponding funds in the budget, the research network can be extended to all suitable educational institutions worldwide.[399]

7.3.8 International education policy

In cooperation with the Ministry of Foreign Affairs, the Ministry of Education pursues an international education policy. In neighbouring countries, the domestic mother tongue is promoted as a foreign language through the PASCH[400] partner school initiative between comprehensive schools. There are also foreign exchanges and language exchanges with partner cities around the world.[401] In the course of communitarisation, educational qualifications are first

395 Ministry of Labour - 20.7.5 Innovation auditor, Ministry of Innovation - 4 Innovation Agency
396 Ministry of Innovation - 7 Technology Policy, 8.2.8 Investigation by the Patent Office
397 Ministry of Innovation - 3.2 International Innovation Policy, 5.1 Continental Cooperation
398 Ministry of Innovation - 5.4 State research projects
399 Ministry of Education - 11.7.1 Research community
400 https://www.pasch-net.de/de/index.html
401 Ministry of Education - 9.16 Foreign exchange, 9.15.2.17 Languages

standardised before curricula and educational programmes can be standardised and adapted to the specialisation of a region.[402] In all reforms, it must be left up to the learners to decide when they want to learn which knowledge using which learning method.

The Knowledge Directory is also made available on the Internet so that the contents can be translated and learned worldwide. In cooperation with the Ministry of Foreign Affairs, foreigners can participate in the filming of the Knowledge Directory.

Foreign comprehensive schools whose degrees are recognised inland are considered schools abroad. The International Council of Ministers of Education is responsible for the recognition of foreign degrees and coordinates its action with the Institute of Education.[403] State funding of educational institutions abroad is not permitted until the Ministries of Education of the Member States are communitarised.

7.3.9 International family policy

The Ministry of Foreign Affairs, in cooperation with the Ministry of Family Affairs, takes care of international children, youths, leisure, senior citizens and family policy. Events are held simultaneously in several participating countries for individual population groups and exchange programmes are established. Contact is established between similar associations and clubs via the embassies and the Foreign Office.

In the course of communitarisation, the rights for children, youths, unmated persons, families and senior citizens are unified. Until then, the rules for partnering, marriage, adoption, parenting and suicide of the country where a person is located apply.

Foreigners are subject to domestic marriage contract law as long as they have not drawn up a marriage contract themselves and deposited it in a domestic Registry Office.[404] Domestic citizens who live abroad are subject to the marriage law of that country as long as no other laws apply in the foreign country.

---

402 Ministry of Education - 11.6.8 Higher education degrees
403 Ministry of Education - 4.8.2 Foreigner recognition
404 Ministry of Family Affairs - 7.4.1 Marriage contract

In the case of adoption of a domestic child by foreign citizens or of a foreign child by domestic citizens, the Foreign Office and the embassy in the affected country are responsible for preventing trafficking in human beings.[405]

In voting with the Ministry of Family Affairs, the Ministry of Foreign Affairs ensures international standards in sport and the fight against doping in competitive sport[406] . The controls are carried out by private agencies. The Ministry of Foreign Affairs, in cooperation with the Ministry of Family Affairs, ensures the international exchange of artists and authors and, in voting with the Ministry of Innovation, communitarisation of copyright.[407]

The communitarisation of children's rights has already progressed through the United Nations Convention on the Rights of the Child[408] , because almost all member states of the United Nations have incorporated the Convention on the Rights of the Child into their national laws. In the next step of communitarisation, the legal texts on the right of the child[409] , which implement the United Nations Convention on the Rights of the Child, will be made identical.

7.3.10 International health policy

The Ministry of Foreign Affairs maintains a representation at the World Health Organization (WHO)[410] , which is in constant contact with the Foreign Department of the Ministry of Health[411] . The WHO is the initial communitarisation of the world's Ministries of Health. It and its agencies pursue the goals of improving global health conditions and reducing or eradicating diseases, especially infectious diseases. The representative coordinates the foreign policy dimension of global health issues with the responsible ministries. The Minister of Health, in voting with the Minister of Foreign

---

405 Ministry of Family Affairs - 7.6.5 Adoption
406 Ministry of Family Affairs - 9.3 Sport
407 Ministry of Innovation - 7.2.3 Copyright
408 https://www.unicef.org/child-rights-convention
409 Ministry of Family Affairs - 8.1 Children's rights
410 https://www.who.int/
411 Ministry of Health - 2.4 Foreign Department

Affairs, ensures the communitarisation of health legislation concerning medical licensing, medical care and health insurance.[412]

The Ministry of Foreign Affairs ensures the forwarding of domestic data on diseases and related health problems for the International Classification of Diseases (ICD)[413] . In voting with the Ministry of Health, the standards for the classification are harmonised internationally.

Requirements for the internationally active pharmaceutical industry and its controls will be standardised in the course of communitarisation and adapted to the highest safety standards.

7.3.10.1 Foreign environmental policy

The representation of the Ministry of Foreign Affairs at the United Nations maintains a representative for the sustainable development goals of the 2030 Agenda.[414] In cooperation with the responsible ministries, examples of domestic implementation of the sustainable development goals are presented and visits to the example location are arranged for interested foreigners.

Poverty reduction is driven by Barter Economy Economic Zones[415] and Social Villages with Planned Economy[416] . Inequality is reduced through peaceful separation or dismantled through universal rights. In cultural protection areas and through municipal laws, like can join like. All those entitled to vote who are affected are given equal admission to digital direct democratic forms of political participation.[417]

In the course of communitarisation, the standards for environmental protection and product safety, including their

412 Ministry of Health - 5 Health care
413 https://www.who.int/standards/classifications/classification-of-diseases
414 https://www.2030agenda.de/de/publication/die-agenda-2030 https://www.un.org/humansecurity/agenda-2030/
415 Ministry of Barter Economy - 10 economic sectors, 4 economic policy, 9 enterprise policy, 16 state services
416 Ministry of Planned Economy - 5 Economic policy
417 Ministry of State Organisation - 8.1 Nationals, 11.5.7 Cultural protection areas for minority protection

auditors and quality seals[418] , will be harmonised. The highest safety standard is decisive in the unification process. The standards for environmental protection and product safety must also be observed by domestic citizens abroad and by their providers. Violations are tried before a domestic court.[419] The embassies and consulates support the domestic authorities in their investigative work.

The Ministry of Foreign Affairs ensures international cooperation on marine protection in all available international bodies in order to standardise limits for pollution from fisheries, sewage and waste.[420]

The Ministry of Foreign Affairs, in cooperation with the Health Agency, is working towards international standardisation of requirements and measures to measure and adapt to climate change.[421]

The Ministry of Foreign Affairs, in voting and in cooperation with the Ministry of Infrastructure, promotes sustainable resource use. This is done through a circular economy[422] , renewable energy and storage capacities, transport routes powered by electricity, pipelines for raw materials and water, biodiversity through permaculture[423] , and urban development where buildings are insulated and equipped to support their own electricity.[424]

7.3.11 International economic policy[425]

The Ministry of Foreign Affairs ensures compliance with the constitutional principles of international economic, financial and trade policy. Accordingly, these policy areas may only be

---

418 Ministry of Labour - 20.7.4.2 Seal of Approval, 17.7.4 Seal of Quality
419 Ministry of Health - 6.4 Product safety, 6.6 Environmental protection
420 Ministry of Health - 6.5.4 Marine Protection
421 Ministry of Health - 6.7 Climate change
422 Ministry of Health - 6.7.2.1 Circular economy
423 Ministry of Labour - 19.8.7 Nature-based agriculture: permaculture
424 Ministry of Infrastructure - 4.3 Raw materials, 4.9.2 Waste disposal, 6 Networks, 8 Traffic, 9.7 Energy supply, 5.3 Building specifications
425 §162,4 foreign affairs, §196,3,4 spatial planning, §225,1,5-8 foreign economic policy: BV Art.101

exposed to international competition in the economic form of the Free Market Economy.

International economic policy is characterised by trade agreements that regulate the foreign trade of goods, services, companies and real estate. The regularisations must be approved by a majority of the affected ministries and the people.

The Ministry of Free Market Economy, in cooperation with the Ministry of Foreign Affairs, promotes the capacity for foreign trade. Companies can obtain advice and support from the Company Auditing Agency and the Foreign Trade Agency for a fee. Associations and chambers of commerce can hold trade fairs on the premises of embassies and consulates if they pay appropriate fees.

In order to compete internationally with the Social Market Economy, the same regulations must apply to companies in the countries involved, as well as an equal standard of living. In addition, joint economic activity is limited to companies that promote sustainable development.[426]

The Barter Economy and Planned Economy only conduct economic, financial and trade policy with other barter economies and planned economies. The only exceptions are People's Innovation Company, Innovation Enterprise and Experimental Enterprise.[427]

7.3.11.1 International economic cooperation

The Organization for Economic Cooperation and Development (OECD)[428] is being pursued in the respect to ensure that common standards are regulated equally in the laws of all member states. The Ministry of Labour strives for global harmonisation of living standards and economic performance. To this end, it imposes entry bans on skilled workers and import and export restrictions on goods and services needed for development in their home countries. If

426Ministry of Social Market Economy - 15 Foreign trade
427Ministry of Planned Economy - 10.6 Innovation Enterprise, 10.8 Experimental Enterprise, Ministry of Innovation - 10 People's Innovation Company
428http://www.oecd.org/

tariffs are levied for development aid, these tariffs flow through the Ministry of Foreign Affairs into development aid.

7.3.11.2 Foreign trade control

Customs is responsible for foreign trade controls[429] and the Ministry of Labour is responsible for foreign trade control law[430] . The Ministry of Foreign Affairs is prohibited from authorising any export of weapons of war and state-subsidised goods and services. The state subsidy may be in the form of funds or services. The people also have the right to ban the export of weapons and food as soon as, after a quorum of 40% in the subsequent voting, a majority is in favour of the ban. The referendum question must also include a choice on the time period of the ban.

7.3.11.3 Real estate sector

The international real estate sector is limited to renting or subletting land. Foreigners persons or companies are not allowed to purchase land in the inland territory. Foreign companies trading in or renting out real estate are not allowed to participate in the domestic housing market. In the course of communitarisation, the real estate sector becomes equally possible for all citizens of the Member States in the middle ring.

7.3.11.4 Agency for foreign trade

The Ministry of Foreign Affairs operates the Foreign Trade Agency in its capital city.[431] It advertises foreign buyers or company partners and, with the help of the Company Auditing Agency, audits them before placing them with domestic companies in the Social Market Economy and Planned Economy.

---

429 Ministry of Security - 8 Customs
430 Ministry of Labour - 10.3 Foreign Trade Regulations
431 https://www.gtai.de/gtai-de

The domestic companies of the Social Market Economy and Planned Economy are provided with the necessary economic information from the embassy or consulates about the affected countries. This includes the market development of individual sectors, current tenders, the current legal situation for each individual case and customs regulations. The agency's scope of services also includes advancing a company's technology policy by searching internationally for innovations offered by foreigner companies. Social Market Economy and Planned Economy companies gain admission to the Foreign Trade Agency through the innovation auditors and business consultants of the Planned Economy.[432] Social Market Economy and Planned Economy companies can access the same services as Free Market Economy companies, but pay less or no fees.

The Ministry of Foreign Affairs offers the international manager training programme[433] for domestic small and medium-sized enterprises. The programme is free of charge for companies in the Planned Economy and Social Market Economy, but there is a charge for companies in the Free Market Economy. In it, tailor-made contacts are established with foreign companies via the embassies and consulates to ensure international fair and sustainable business.

7.3.11.5 International trade

The Ministry of Foreign Affairs may only approve international trade policies that do not cause damage to domestic and foreign citizens. It implements trade policy instruments[434] of the other ministries, limits foreign services[435] , protects intellectual property[436] and operates a customs policy[437] to avert damage and purchasing power differentials between

---

432 Ministry of Labour - 20.7.5 innovation auditor, 20.7.7 business consultant
433 https://www.bmwi.de/Redaktion/DE/Artikel/Aussenwirtschaft/managerfortbildungsprogramm.html
434 Ministry of Labour - 10.3.1 Restrictions
435 Ministry of Labour - 16.11 Guest work
436 Ministry of Innovation - Technology Policy
437 Ministry of Labour - 10.3.2 Tariffs

trading partners.

The United Nations Commission on International Trade Law (UNCITRAL)[438] aims to standardise international trade law. It thus forms the basis for global trade law as soon as the ministries of labour and economics are communitarised in the middle ring. In the course of communitarisation, foreign economic policy[439] of the ministries of economy must be unified, which includes the establishment of further economic forms. The responsibility of arbitration courts will be transferred to the International Court of Justice, which will then no longer be responsible only for states, but also for citizens and companies.

The World Trade Organization (WTO)[440] is an international organisation with 164 members, limited to international trade. The ministries affected are the Ministries of Labour and Free Market Economy, with the WTO's influence applied only to the Ministry of Free Market Economy. In the course of communitarisation, the WTO is incorporated into the International Union of the United Nations as part of the international Ministry of Free Market Economy. The other ministries of economy follow only once their ministries are communitarised in the middle ring.

7.3.12 International labour policy

The Ministry of Labour pursues an international labour policy in voting with the Ministry of Foreign Affairs.[441] It ensures compliance with or abolition of applicable international agreements on international labour law and maritime labour law. It may extend or restrict the validity to individual economic forms. The decisive factor is that the requirements are met in at least one economic form. The ministries of foreign affairs and labour of the member states jointly set international labour law. They observe the previous and establish the new

---

438 https://uncitral.un.org/
439 Ministries of Economy - Foreign Trade
440 https://www.wto.org/
441 Ministry of Labour - 10.3 Foreign trade regulations, 16.11 Guest work

principles of the International Labor Organization (ILO)[442]. The aim is to ensure that social justice, human rights and labour rights are respected in international labour policy when it comes to the export and import of goods, the departure and arrival of foreign workers, the sale of domestic companies to foreigners or the purchase of foreign companies by domestic citizens.

The Ministry of Foreign Affairs, in voting with the Ministry of Labour, ensures that international labour policy is aligned with international economic and trade policy. This includes rights for entrepreneurs and traders as well as international rights for employees and consumers.

International labour policy is pursued by the Ministry of Foreign Affairs in the WTO, as well as in UNCITRAL and the OECD. The Organization for Economic Cooperation and Development (OECD)[443] is an international organisation with 37 member states that are more advanced in economic policy communitarisation. The ministries affected are Labour, Education, Integration, Health, Innovation, Finance, Social Market Economy and Free Market Economy. In the course of communitarisation, the OECD forms the basis for an international Ministry of Labour and is incorporated into the International Union of the United Nations. The Ministry of Foreign Affairs' representation at the OECD coordinates cooperation with foreign ministries. In the course of communitarisation, it ensures the transfer of the OECD to the International Union of the United Nations and the merger with the representation to the United Nations.

7.3.12.1 International labour law

The Minister for Foreign Affairs may restrict economic activity with foreign countries if different labour laws apply in the affected country or if the validity of rights for employers and employees is unequal internationally. Equal validity is achieved when economic, trade and labour laws are unified. Equal enforcement is achieved when the ministries of economics

442https://www.ilo.org/global/lang--en/index.htm
443http://www.oecd.org/

and labour are communitarised.

Part of international labour rights is the development of international labour unions for all industries engaged in business and trade in the international market. In the course of communitarisation, there must be a corresponding international labour union for each industry involved in the world market, which negotiates minimum wages and occupational safety measures in collective labour agreements. The necessary international labour rights include the Ministry of Labour's requirements for employee protection, labour market policy and pensions.[444] No economic activity may be conducted with foreigners without compliance with these rights. Exceptions can be made by the people in the Ministry of Free Market Economy.

7.3.12.2 International cooperation in vocational education and training

International cooperation in VET begins with the standardisation and recognition of foreign educational qualifications.[445] International VET is achieved through the standardisation of VET measures[446] . Internships or university semesters abroad are made possible for domestic citizens and foreigners as long as uniform conditions apply to interns and students in both countries. The Ministry of Foreign Affairs ensures the necessary agreements in voting with the Ministries of Labour and Education. At their own request, domestic citizens can study or complete internships in any country, provided the affected inland agrees.

7.3.12.3 International division of labour

It must be possible for the basic supply of each population to be guaranteed by its own country. Furthermore, the division of labour can also take place between several states if the

---

444 Ministry of Labour - 16 Employee protection, 12 Employment Office, 21 Pension
445 Ministry of Education - 4.8.2 Foreigner recognition
446 Ministry of Labour - 11.2 Vocational training

Ministries of Economics and Labour of these states formulate international trade agreements for this purpose and submit them to their peoples for voting.

7.3.12.4 International labour market integration

The United Nations is in the outer ring of integration of an International Union at the Ministry of Labour. All agreements are not legally binding because there are no common laws, courts and elected governments. Companies can voluntarily follow the rules for Corporate Social Responsibility (CSR)[447] . Those who do not comply with international agreements cannot be punished.

The Ministry of Labour forces states and companies to comply with the agreements by imposing import and export restrictions on assets, goods and services, as well as entry restrictions.

The further integration of the international community of states will only be advanced when all Continental Union member states are in the inner ring of integration and have given themselves a common constitution. The aim of the united states of the continent is not to admit individual states from the whole world, but to push forward the unification of other states into continental federal states. The means to build up this pressure is again a restriction on the mobility of assets, persons, goods and services.

7.3.12.5 International agricultural policy

In principle, the Ministry of Foreign Affairs undertakes to prevent any export of food subsidised by state funds or services. It also prevents the import of food from countries where the population is suffering from hunger. The Ministry of Foreign Affairs is trying to reach this agreement with an increasing number of countries.

447https://www.unido.org/our-focus/advancing-economic-competitiveness/competitive-trade-capacities-and-corporate-responsibility/corporate-social-responsibility-market-integration/what-csr

7.3.12.5.1 Deep-sea fishing

International agriculture takes place mainly in the oceans, where the peoples of the world fish together. In order to protect this environment, which is so far no one's national territory, joint sea fisheries management is being sought in the United Nations. The Ministry of Foreign Affairs strives for sustainable marine fisheries that do not harm the stocks in the oceans. The responsibilities of the International Whaling Commission (IWC)[448] are increasingly being expanded to include more species of marine life. In the course of communitarisation, fish production in aquacultures is being pushed forward until it can replace sea fishing in terms of quantity. All catches that may then still be fished from the oceans are those that do not thrive in aquaculture and cannot be replaced by fish from aquaculture. In international waters, fishing will only be allowed with longlines[449] that are equipped with tracking devices and can be located after being broken off. Fish caught otherwise may not be imported into the domestic market. Compliance with the requirements is monitored on a random basis. When ships are overflown, satellites take photos that are automatically analysed. If inadmissible fishing methods or the dumping of waste in the sea are discovered, the footage is forwarded to the International Criminal Court and charges are filed. Ship owners or states in which the ship is registered can be banned from entering domestic ports or trading with the inland.

7.3.12.5.2 World food supply

The communitarisation of agriculture is being promoted by the Ministry of Labour in cooperation with the Ministry of Foreign Affairs. In order to reduce food prices, increase availability and protect the environment, permaculture[450] is being introduced on an industrial scale on previous farmland in all countries, if possible, and is becoming increasingly

---

448https://iwc.int/home
449https://de.wikipedia.org/wiki/Langleinenfischerei
450https://en.wikipedia.org/wiki/Permaculture

automated.[451] The Ministry of Foreign Affairs, in cooperation with the Ministries of Labour and Digital Affairs, promotes world food. Satellite imagery is being used to automatically evaluate all regions of the world and identify cultivation opportunities for permaculture. Existing soil conditions, plants and animals in the region are automatically recognised as far as is possible with the imagery. Based on the data, a management of forest and field with permaculture including necessary extension work, such as heat traps with ponds or irrigation possibilities, is automatically created.

The World Food Programme[452] is transforming its service to increasingly provide crop plans and seed packets designed for each region. Persons in need of food report their place of residence and whereabouts. They then receive a cultivation plan and a seed packet for the corresponding area. Name and address data are stored. If another person comes from the same area, they receive a request to cooperate with their neighbour who already has a plan and seeds. If the soil conditions are too nutrient-poor, instructions on how to make Terra Preta[453] are attached to the plan. If there is too little water available, equipment to build air water filters[454] will be supplied. The World Food Programme will accompany the affected areas with food supplies until the permaculture is mature enough to provide sufficient food after about 4 years. Accordingly, the food supplies are reduced and eventually stopped altogether.

The Ministry of Foreign Affairs' contribution is the programme for automatic evaluation and creation of cultivation plans, as well as a seed bank and starter kits for setting up a new seed bank. For follow-up, the Ministry of Digital Affairs is creating a website where seeds can be exchanged and yields can be saved, sold or exchanged. The data is analysed and high-yielding plants at a location with certain textures are included in the cultivation plans.

451 Ministry of Labour - 19.8.7 Nature-based agriculture: permaculture
452 https://de.wfp.org/
453 https://de.wikipedia.org/wiki/Terra_preta
454 https://www.scinexx.de/news/technik/wasser-aus-der-wuestenluft/

7.3.13 International financial policy[455]

The Ministry of Foreign Affairs regulates the influence of foreign assets in international financial policy. Foreigner influence on the state budget must be prevented. The state may not lend money from other states, nor from foreigners. Its only source of credit is the issue of government bonds to its own citizens. In this way, other states can also gradually reduce their debt, because the interest payments to their population strengthen their purchasing power.

In the course of communitarisation, the international finance economy is initially only permitted in the free market economies. Only when uniform laws on taxes, the Company Auditing Authority as well as the Financial Supervisory Authority[456] apply in the states involved, can the Ideas Stock Exchange and the People's Stock Exchange[457] also be made accessible to citizens of the member states.

The International Monetary Fund (IMF)[458] becomes responsible for the stability of the internationalised currencies. inland, only the Note-issuing Bank of the Ministry of Free Market Economy is affected. In the course of communitarisation, the IMF is incorporated as a body into the International Union of the United Nations, in the outer ring of the International Ministry of Finance. Voting rights will be allocated democratically and not by capital contribution, and the responsible politicians will be directly elected. In future, states are to lend money from their population and not from other states through the IMF.

In the course of communitarisation, poorer countries catch up and living standards are equalised. Without capital exports, independently viable domestic markets can quickly use the latest technologies to copy the economic cycles of the industrialised nations. For entrance into the inner ring of the united states of the world, freedom from debt and a budget surplus of at least 5% of the Gross Domestic Product

---

455§225,9 Foreign Trade Policy, §152,1,5 Tariffs: BV Art.133
456Ministry of Labour - 18.3 Financial Supervisory Authority
457Ministry of Finance - 11.8 People's Stock Exchange, 11.9 Ideas Stock Exchange
458https://www.imf.org/en/Home

are necessary. These budget surpluses will be used to find and colonise new habitable planets.

7.3.13.1 Budget of International Unions

For the time being, the Ministry of Foreign Affairs treats tariffs as revenues to its own national budget. In the course of communitarisation, it is used to finance the budget of the United Nations. Since tariffs are supposed to be incurred whenever they compensate for inequalities, they are invested by the United Nations in development programmes that can reduce inequalities. Negotiations on inequalities and their reduction are conducted by the responsible Ministers of the involved countries and the peoples vote on the results of the negotiations. A budget vote is held to distribute the revenues, with the project amount reserved for development programmes.[459] The assets in the IMF are used as savings for the United Nations budget and distributed by the donor countries to profitable projects. The process is carried out digitally and publicly with the tax game .[460]

7.3.13.2 State bankruptcy

The Ministry of Foreign Affairs is involved in the international financial architecture in voting and cooperation with the Ministries of Finance, Labour and Economic Affairs. With the help of the embassies, the Foreign Office prepares economic country analyses to assess the solvency of countries and their entrepreneurs.

International financial and currency policy is designed to prevent or control sovereign defaults. In a controlled resolution, all debts are cancelled and all foreign trade is interrupted for at least 10 years. The countries must then undergo a currency reform and learn to survive independently in their own countries. Only when they produce surpluses again that they can sell, will they be involved in world trade again.

---

459 Ministry of Finance - 9.5 Budget vote
460 Ministry of Finance - 9.6 Tax game

7.3.13.3 International tax law

The Ministry of Foreign Affairs ensures international tax law in voting with the Ministry of Finance. As a confidence-building measure, an exchange of information and international cooperation in the area of taxation will be initiated with as many states as possible.[461] States that refuse and do not expel a Gross Domestic Product can be excluded from international policy cooperation and trade with the inland, as can states and companies that maintain relations with these states.

An initial unification of tax law can be found in the OECD's double taxation agreements.[462] The Ministry of Foreign Affairs advocates tax unification for business taxes and value added taxes, and different tax rates between economic forms, but uniform tax rates worldwide for all economic forms and value added tax. In the course of communitarisation, an increasingly larger share of business taxes is paid out as Unconditional Basic Income as automation increases.[463]

7.4 United States of the Continents[464]

The Ministry of Foreign Affairs shall ensure, within the limits of its powers in international policy, the establishment of international unions on the continents and agreement on the extension of the areas to be designated as continents.

The concept of continents here is more comparable to the concept of a geologically more or less delimited, uniformly large and culturally similar area. The external borders of the territories correspond to the national borders of the member states located on the periphery of the territory. Each area should contain as much land area, sea area and population as possible in order to avoid distribution conflicts. It is precisely at border regions that states, or even individual municipalities, can decide to belong to one continent or the other. In doing so, they determine which International Union they would like

---

461 Ministry of Security - 8.3.1 Tax Investigation abroad
462 https://www.oecd.org/berlin/publikationen/oecd-musterabkommenz
urvermeidungvondoppelbesteuerung.htm
463 Ministry of Finance - 6 Unconditional Basic Income
464 §168.3 World peace

to become a member of.

In the medium term, states on one continent worldwide are to unite in 25 to 100 years to form the United States of their continent. They are to administer their land and sea territory in a self-sufficient, sustainable and environmentally friendly way. Self-sufficient means that the humans living together on one continent could survive without the rest of the world. Sustainable means that the humans live on their continent in such a way that they maintain at least the same standard of living for all future generations. Environmentally friendly means that the people on a continent, through their way of life, do not deprive themselves, the humans on the rest of the world or the global nature of their future livelihood.

7.4.1 Procedure of unification

The procedure for communitarisation of states and federal states can be taken over by states from the Continental Union, developed by states themselves or founded an International Union and follow the three rings of integration. Worldwide, the United States of the Continents are to develop from the international unions during this time, namely America, Africa, Europe, Arapersia and Asia. The United States of the Continents will then begin to make first diplomatic, later democratic agreements, which will then lead to the International Union of the Earth.

Normally, at least two foreign ministers establish an International Union for their continent. The proposal is made as to the maximum number of states on the continent that should participate. It is up to them whether the states named want to participate or not. They are automatically members of the outer ring from the moment of foundation. All member states can propose further states to be involved in the International Union of the continent.

The states of the continents first communitarise in the outer and middle ring until they unify in the inner ring. The aim of integration is to carry out communitarisation and unification at a speed that is linked to the speed of integration of the peoples involved and their standard of living. Communitarisation normally proceeds as follows. First, uniform laws are gradually created in an increasing number of ministries. Then uniform programmes and politicians are elected for agencies and ministries. Finally, a constitution is established that describes how the uniform political structures, processes and contents should look.

The Ministry of Free Market Economy is communitarised at the outset. To this end, trade agreements will be concluded to ensure balanced imports and exports as well as uniform standards for goods, services, labour and environmental safety. Fair trade should enable states with lower living standards to catch up. If not all member states are democracies, trade agreements can be concluded diplomatically. All peoples who are democracies must vote on the treaties. The second ministry to receive increasingly uniform rules in all member states, i.e. to be communitarised, is the Ministry of Labour. After that, the other ministries for economy and innovation can follow.

To reduce state expenditure on defence and security, peace treaties can be concluded immediately after the establishment of the International Union, and armies and military budgets can be merged and downsized. To reduce expenditure even more, border controls and tariffs at internal borders can be eliminated. However, part of the saved costs must be invested in policing and protecting the external borders.

After that, the other eleven ministries can be communitarised independently in time. It is only advisable to communitarise individual authorities from the ministries if their head is directly elected and if all national authorities are closed in favour of an international authority.

7.4.2 National territories

In the medium term, the United States of the Continents is to be formed all over the world. Each time a state joins, the constitution can be discussed and formulated anew, but should remain true to the model of the dynamic media democracy[465]. The United States of the Continents seek peace treaties with

____

465 Ministry of State Organisation - 5 Theories of Dynamic Media Democracy

all other clubs and especially with other unified states of the Continents.

The Convention on the Law of the Sea[466] regulates all uses of the oceans and from where the national borders on the coasts begin. In the course of communitarisation, each continent is given its share of the world's oceans to use. The priority requirements for use are set by all the states of the world in the Convention on the Law of the Sea.

7.4.2.1 World map of the medium term

United States of America	Alaska to Argentina
United states of Europe	Portugal to Russia
United States of Arabia and Persia	Turkey to India
United States of Asia	Mongolia to Australia
United States of Africa	Egypt to South Africa

The United States gradually unifies. In the process, artificial names are created that carry the names of the continents. A unification of the continents could bear names such as AmEurope, AmEurAsia, AmEurAsiArapersia or even AmEurAsiArapersika. The states must first become democratic, then direct democratic and finally agree to the common constitution of the world.

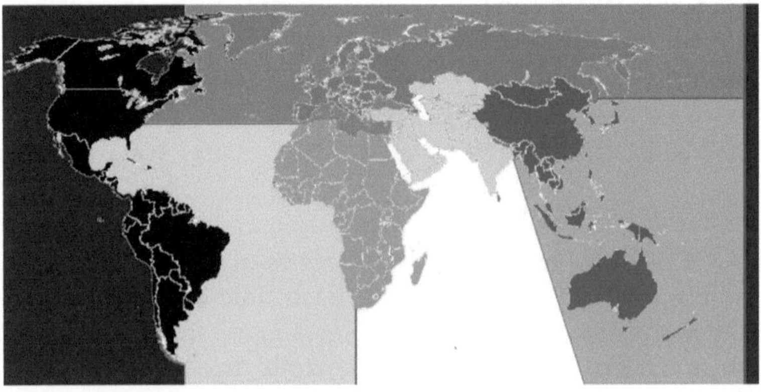

466https://eur-lex.europa.eu/legal-content/EN/
TXT/?uri=CELEX:21998A0623(01)

This map is intended to represent an impression of the communitarisation of the Earth's states. What such a world map will ultimately look like will be decided by the peoples over generations. The goal remains the united states of the world. How this goal is achieved is to be decided directly and democratically by all the citizens of the earth.

7.4.3 Culture

For the protection of minorities, cultural protection areas[467] are chosen by the population. If possible, the local traditional culture or subcultures typical of a country should be cared for there. The citizens of a municipality[468] decide how far they want to exclude themselves.

Through the new municipal policy, cities and municipalities can form alliances in order to be able to practise a different way of life in their place of residence in this region after a referendum. Since the monopoly on the use of force must lie with the democratically controlled state, the ministries of security and justice cannot be administered municipally. In the medium term, the territorial claim to parts of the earth can be dismantled within the thought structures of the humans, with municipal territories and economic forms protecting minorities.

7.4.4 Integration

Member states in the International Union of a continent should be a community of peoples with a majority of the same faith. By no means do the peoples in the unified states have to be ethnically pure or exclusively of one religion, but they should form the majority. Immigration from countries that are not candidates for membership of the continent's International Union will be restricted to tourist visas and asylum procedures until there is a uniform standard of living in all regions. The Ministry of Integration ensures that new residents, regardless

467 Ministry of Integration - 6.3 Cultural protection area
468 Ministry of State Organisation - 11.5 Municipal policy

of which parts of the continent they come from, are well integrated into the local community and can quickly make domestic friends.[469] It also runs asylum seeker support, policy dialogue with and regularisation of religions, and referendums on quotas of foreign nationals on the continent.

Each federal state in the inner ring elects its lead religion, but otherwise strictly separates state and church. Religion is seen as divine policy, nations as state policy. The God of the existing religions is not democratic, so religions in democracies cannot take over state functions. At most, they can shape values that the population wants enshrined in their laws.

7.4.5 Infrastructure

In the long term, the infrastructure is designed to connect all continents of the earth with each other on land, at sea, in the air and through space. The standard for the construction of the long-distance transport routes is set jointly by as many countries as possible.[470] In the medium term, the United States of the Continents should be connected by underground routes.[471] Goods, electricity, data, water, liquids and gases will be moved across the continent at high speed in this way. Transport across the oceans will be handled by oversized ships. Maglev trains run above ground for passenger transport and connect major cities. Roads run through cities and paths for cyclists and pedestrians connect towns and cities. Airspace is used to transport persons and oversized goods that do not fit into the underground track. Space is used for persons to travel long distances around the earth or through space to other planets.

7.4.6 Innovation

Innovation is necessary to raise the standard of living as quickly as possible within an area. If innovation is executed in a division of labour, more different research areas can be

---

469 Ministry of Integration - 6 Integration, 7.7 Integration measures
470 Ministry of Infrastructure - 8 Traffic
471 Ministry of Infrastructure - 6.2 Underground networks

covered more quickly. In the course of specialisation, each country chooses a focus and coordinates it with the other countries on its continent. This makes it easier for specialists to find their way around and for research institutions to set priorities.

For example, Germany has a long tradition of building means of transport. Therefore, Germany is taking on the development of technology in the field of transport. As a continent-wide field of technology, bionics, biotechnology and biochemistry are being pursued in all states of the united states of the continent. For example, chloroplasts in muscle cells are to replace electric motors, data lines are to grow from nerve cells, axioms and synapses, or chitin and horn are to replace plastic and grow in any desired shape.

Other unified states should be able to occupy other fields of technology, such as electricity, data processing, food production, recycling and valorisation. Through joint specialisation, faster progress should be made in all specialist departments and all states should occupy profitable business fields.

7.4.7 Finance

It is crucial for the self-sufficiency of each continent not to have any debts to another continent and at the same time to have member states with as little debt as possible. Therefore, individual states can only borrow from their citizens. Government bonds can only be issued to nationals. This means that all interest on debt flows into the domestic economy and strengthens purchasing power and tax revenues.

In order to keep the value of money stable despite economic growth, productivity is increased by investing in innovations. Accordingly, credit is only granted to those who want to invest the money in a novelty that is capable of increasing the population's standard of living without damaging others. Loans for consumption are prohibited.

All member states in the United States of the Continents are to draw up a budget with no debts, 5% profits and savings for the coming financial year. In the inner ring of the United

States of the Continents, the budget for all ministries is set in the budget vote[472] from the savings for the coming year. Only what has been saved may be spent in the budget. Withdrawals from current tax revenues must be approved by referendum.

7.5 United States of the World

The Ministry of Foreign Affairs pursues with its international policy the goal of creating the united states of the world. In the short term, all existing forms of international policy are used, provided they are not democratically rejected by the people or oppose the goal of the united states of the world. Simultaneous communitarisation at continental and international levels is possible if national and continental laws do not conflict with international agreements. International law cannot be applied in a legally effective manner inland as long as it has not been democratically set.

Ideally, laws are so universally accepted that they gain sufficient international consent. Democratic international political structures and processes must first be developed by an International Union before the negotiation of international agreements can be voted on with the affected peoples.

Normally, laws have to be negotiated and compromises have to be found before they can be sufficiently agreed upon. Normally, sufficient agreement cannot be found in all states. That is why at the international level there are different treaties on international regularisations with different numbers of signatory states. In an International Union there are three rings of integration, in which different numbers of member states can be represented.

In exceptional cases, laws are contrary to the global or continental majority opinion. In this case, communitarisation cannot take place until the political structures, processes and contents are democratically aligned. With their speed of integration, the peoples determine how long it will take them to join the united states of the world.

---

472 Ministry of Finance - 9.5 Budget vote

7.5.1 Simultaneous continental and global communitarisation

In the case of simultaneous communitarisation at continental and global levels, there must be no duplication of norms and institutions. Norms are all laws and constitutions of the states as well as international or continental contractually agreed law. Institutions are all authorities and ministries of the states as well as international and continental organisations or unions. The duplication of norms and institutions creates confusion through an unclear legal situation, opaque intertwining of responsibilities, chains of legitimacy with unelected politicians and waste of state funds. This must be avoided.

Therefore, democratic norms and institutions always take precedence over diplomatic norms and institutions. This means diplomatic norms and institutions may only exist if there is no comparable democratic option. Diplomats must abide by the democratically set norms of the peoples when negotiating and must have all negotiations voted on by the affected peoples before they come into force. If peoples have already joined together in a continental union, its democratic supranational laws apply. For institutions, this means that international organisations may only create their own agencies if there are no comparable authorities at national or supranational level. International organisations must first establish democratic structures and processes, including separation of powers, before they are allowed to act in an executive and not just advisory capacity.

As a general rule, norms and institutions from the middle ring take precedence over the outer ring. This principle is illustrated by an example on policing. Assuming a member state has its Ministry of Security communitarised in the middle ring of the International Union and in the outer ring of the United Nations, the following responsibilities would apply in the case of an international arrest warrant. The continental police lead the investigation, use the continental police officers of the member states and are supported by Interpol with data.

Furthermore, global norms and institutions take precedence over continental and national norms and institutions as long as norms are democratically set and institutions are democratically run. This means that similar national laws, continental and if possible international, are unified. For institutions, this means that institutions with similar tasks are merged. National institutions with similar functions are abandoned in favour of continental and, if possible, international institutions. Continental institutions are abandoned and their responsibility shifted to international institutions as soon as a democratic separation of powers can be guaranteed and responsible politicians are directly elected. The principle is that the more states have the same laws and common institutions, the better.

7.5.2 Long-term perspective[473]

The Ministry of Foreign Affairs is ensuring that the United Nations is transformed into an International Union. This is intended to make increasingly responsible ministers, rather than heads of state and government, responsible for policy in their remit. Communitarisation is taking place gradually, although in the current initial state there are already beginnings on the outer ring through international law and international organisations. With the help of the international unions of the United States of the Continents, ministries can be communitarised more easily in the middle ring. In the long term, all states of the world communitarise in the inner ring of a global International Union towards the united states of the world.

7.5.2.1 Survival of humankind

In the long term, a federal world society is to be established in 100 to 200 years that is able to administer itself directly and democratically and to colonise new planets in peace. The highest goal of all humans and policies must be to preserve the human species in the universe at all costs. This goal is what all living beings on earth have pursued on this planet and so should humans do, in their legacy to their mother earth, even

---

473 §168,1,6 World peace

if one day the earth has already been destroyed by the universe. It is decisive that, according to the current state of science, it is certain that the Earth is transient or that conditions will occur that will make human life on Earth impossible or considerably more difficult for fewer humans. Therefore, the united states of the world commit themselves to protect the Earth by all means and at the same time to colonise new planets in order to ensure the survival of humanity in the universe.

7.5.2.2 World peace

In order to ensure lasting peace on earth, the constitution of the united states of the world must contain a prohibition of war and killing as follows. War between states and humans is prohibited. Humans are forbidden to kill each other unless there is the express treaty consent of all participants.[474] Conflicts must be resolved democratically. If necessary, two parties to a conflict are separated from each other in time and place until they can live in peace, if necessary still separated, on earth. Demarcation possibilities exist by shifting responsibilities of ministries to the municipal level through a subsidiarity vote or cultural protection areas.[475]

7.5.2.3 World government

In the long term, there should be no other political levels except the municipal level with thousands of municipalities, i.e. cities and municipalities, and a global level with one capital city for each ministry. Government meetings will rotate between municipal council buildings, stadiums, TV studios, on the street with People's Motor Vehicles[476] or airships with a glass cabinet that can be lowered to hold committees.

The dynamic media democracy opens up sufficient electoral possibilities and direct elections for offices. Heads of state and government and their diplomats are replaced by directly elected

---

474 Ministry of Family Affairs - 11.2 Suicide
475 Ministry of State Organisation - 10.3 Subsidiarity coordination, 11.5 Municipal policy, Ministry of Integration - 6.3 Cultural protection area
476 Ministry of Media - 7.1.1 People's Motor Vehicle

politicians, i.e. ministers, their municipal deputies, heads of important agencies and judges. Each additional political level makes it increasingly difficult for voters to correctly assign political responsibilities. In the dynamic media democracy, every political mandate is linked to a political responsibility, so that voters can punish political misconduct.

7.5.2.4 Global economy

The future should be that trade is conducted between all humans on the globe. Everyone should do what they can do best and use what the earth offers in their environment. The highest commandment of all economic activity is the use of the earth without exploiting it to such an extent that it is ruined. Ruinous economic activity, in which more is consumed than can grow back, or environmental pollution is practised, is therefore forbidden. Violations are punished by the global monopoly of force of the world state.

The four economic forms remain worldwide, but the Free Market Economy receives laws that apply to worldwide trade. The Social Market Economy and Planned Economy create more laws to maintain their standards. The national currencies of the Social Market Economy merge into the "safe currency" with stable value and the international currencies of the Free Market Economy merge into the "free currency" with fluctuating value. The working hours of the Planned Economy are maintained. Barter is taxed outside the Barter Economy Zone and no raw materials may be exported from the Barter Economy Zone, except that the annual renewability of all raw materials remains guaranteed.

All humans receive Unconditional Basic Income[477] , which is earned through the work of machines in companies that pay business taxes. In addition, humans earn money through their inventiveness by registering industrial property rights on innovations and can receive royalties for them over the limited term. After this period, the protection is lifted and the innovation is freely available to mankind.

---

477 Ministry of Finance - 6 Unconditional Basic Income

8 Development aid

The Ministry of Foreign Affairs operates continental and international development aid. While continental development aid aims to equalise living standards in the Continental Union, international development aid acts as humanitarian aid in developing countries. Continental development aid is implemented and financed with the member states of the Continental Union within the framework of structural policy. International development aid is provided with other member states within the framework of United Nations missions. The strategy of development aid remains the same for continental and international development aid. It relies on the assistance of local civil society. It promotes economic, social and democratic structures and supports domestic people in applying democratic processes. In principle, state and religion also remain separate in development aid. Religious aid organisations can support state development aid, but are not supported in their own projects. The use of state development aid funds must remain democratically controlled.

Development aid aims to help people help themselves in all areas. These concerns range from governance to agriculture. The focus is on issues that arise in the countries where development aid is to be provided. For example: How do I construct a functioning party system? How do I distribute power? How do I administer an agency? How do I cultivate a field? How do I build a house? How do I start a company? Development aid must never be a monetary payment because money never solves problems, it only pays for services that solve problems. If monetary poverty in a country is too great, microcredits financed by development banks can be an exception. The interest amount must not exceed the inflation rate of the developing country.

The purpose of development aid is to raise the standard of living of all humans to the same level. An equal standard of living means that all the peoples of the world will have the same opportunities to use the state of the art in the future.

8.1 Mode of action

Development aid has three areas of impact, which are also tackled in the following order. First, development aid is given to neighbouring countries around their own whose per capita income is more than 10% lower than their own average. Second, states that have been affected by war or natural disasters receive development aid. Thirdly, development aid is given to countries that have been classified as developing countries, that have been or are affected by imperial exploitation, or that are heavily polluted by industrial overexploitation.
Simultaneous implementation of all three areas of impact would exceed capacities. Only when the international community builds its own capacity does the Ministry of Foreign Affairs manage construction machinery and organise the transport of volunteers to the development area.

8.2 Development Agency

The Development Agency is responsible for implementing development aid. It arranges and manages the construction of technical and social infrastructure. Technical infrastructure means, for example, transport routes, sewers, water, electricity and data lines. Social infrastructure means the establishment of nationwide remit parties as well as local digital administration in the town hall with a marketplace. The marketplace serves as a political meeting place for the citizens of a city. There, direct democratic decisions are to be practised face to face before they take place digitally.
The social infrastructure also includes professionals, namely state administrative staff, teachers in educational institutions for all age groups and doctors for health care facilities. The first generation of skilled personnel completes their training in the industrialised nations and, after returning home, trains the following generations in their own developing country.
Embassies coordinate development aid and contribute to the successful implementation of projects with their knowledge of the language and the country. In cooperation with the Institute for Development, they check whether and what

development aid a country needs and whether the majority of the population there wants to receive the development aid. Embassy staff work with the ministries of labour, education and infrastructure to deploy their staff and materials.

8.3 Institute for development aid

The Institute for Development Aid determines which countries are considered developing countries and examines the conditions there in cooperation with the embassies. In addition, the Institute evaluates all ongoing development aid projects for their results and prospects of success. It publishes its findings annually before the budget vote and prepares assignments for development aid. On the basis of its research findings, projects, measures and strategies are adjusted to maximise their effectiveness.

8.4 Operation sites[478]

The Ministry of Foreign Affairs, in cooperation with the Ministries of Education and Infrastructure, provides the necessary measures for development aid. The Development Agency targets one country at a time. The deployment of personnel and resources is thus concentrated on only one country. This is done until the country has lost its status as a developing country. For example, Poland is currently considered a developing country compared to Germany. This country still has a lower standard of living than Germany and is the immediate neighbour. The development aid groups move on to the next developing country as soon as foreigners who have been trained inland take over. Initially, the development aid is on the road in all underdeveloped regions of their own country to try out their work there. Then the foreign missions begin in the first needy and willing neighbouring country. The more underdeveloped the countries are, the more difficult the work will be. To perfect the procedures, development workers start in countries that are similar but somewhat less developed,

---

478§162.5 Foreign affairs

to learn how to help increasingly less developed states effectively and quickly. In the medium term, development aid expands to include candidates for membership of the united states of the continent. Once all countries that are to join the united states of the continent are developed, the process continues with the neighbouring underdeveloped continent until all countries there have lost their status as developing countries. Where aid is given is first decided by how well the surrounding neighbouring countries are doing, in a circular fashion. In the short and medium term, there is a focus in development aid on equalising living standards across the continent. In the medium term, a strong continent will then help the developing and emerging countries in the neighbouring underdeveloped continent to become ready for an International Union. The advantage of this procedure is to develop more and more countries in such a way that they are able to provide development aid in other countries themselves or join the development aid of another member state.

If all continents of the world implement this kind of development aid at the same time, the global standard of living can be equalised as quickly as possible. Basically, each continent develops itself and then takes care of its neighbouring continent in need, which still has a lower standard of living.

8.4.1 Standard of living

A basic requirement is meant by the standard of living. In the long term, every human should have the possibility to use the state of the art. This includes not freezing to death, starving to death or dying of disease. So you have to be able to earn money at any time. This money can then be used to finance the state of the art in medicine, mobility, real estate and nutrition. The standard of living of one's own population is considered a target in development aid. It should be possible to rise from a simple life in the forest in the Barter Economy, to the Planned Economy in the Social Village, to the People's Innovation Company in the Social Market Economy, and finally to the top management in a globally operating corporation in the Free Market Economy within a lifetime.

The goal of development aid is to equalise all living standards worldwide. Gross Domestic Product, suicide rate, inflation rate, unemployment rate, birth rate and per capita income in national currency are used as references. From these, a quotient is formed for the standard of living[479] so that one can measure how far one is progressing with development aid. As soon as all planned construction and education projects are completed, the development workers move on to the next country.

Development aid helps people to help themselves so that the local population can reach the standard of living of the donor country. Development aid does not, for example, ensure that the Gross Domestic Product is the same inland and in Poland. It merely ensures that the infrastructure and education are at the same level in order to achieve the same Gross Domestic Product per capita in the medium term. The equalisation of lifestyles is not a goal of development aid.

8.5 Conditions for a relief mission

Whether and where a development aid intervention begins is linked to the following three conditions. Only when all three conditions are met is development aid provided. As soon as one condition is no longer fulfilled, development aid is stopped in that country.

First, the foreign minister is responsible for deciding which country should receive development aid. He consults his embassies and his people in a committee and advertises the necessary tax funds at the next budget vote. The people can end any mission by a veto quorum.

Secondly, the embassy from the donor country asks the foreign government whether the development aid is refused, admitted or supported. Approved means development aid without support from state staff or funds. Supported can mean either providing funds from the domestic budget or giving instructions to executive bodies such as the police, military or teachers to actively support development aid in construction activities and education, to secure them and to recruit the

---

479 Ministry of Finance - 10.5 Living Standard Index

cooperation of the population.

Thirdly, ambassadors ask the domestic population whether the development aid is desired. Embassy staff conduct information campaigns informing people about the date and topic of the upcoming voting. Embassy staff put up posters at town halls around the country informing citizens when town hall polling stations open and close. For a week, election workers sit in the town hall polling station and dye one finger blue of all voters who cast their vote on the Ministry of Foreign Affairs voting computer. In addition, 10 election workers walk around the city with voting computers asking citizens to cast their votes. From a majority of 65% of the population, this condition is considered fulfilled.

8.6 Development workers

The staff for development aid comes from the ministries of labour[480] , infrastructure[481] , education[482] and health[483] . The necessary equipment for the staff is ordered by the Development Agency through the Procurement Office or lent out if the ministries can spare the devices.

Volunteers can additionally report to the Foreign Office as development workers. They receive a briefing and travel to the development area together with the state aid workers and freight or independently at their own expense.

8.7 Financing development aid

Financing for development aid comes partly from the state budget and partly from private sponsors or donors. The money from the state budget consists of the revenues from import and export duties for development aid.[484] If further funds

---

480 Ministry of Labour - 20.7.5 innovation auditor, 20.7.7 business consultant

481 Ministry of Infrastructure - 5.8 Construction Team

482 Ministry of Education - 4.11 Teachers

483 Ministry of Health - 4.4 Health auditors of the Company Auditing Agency, 4.5 Institutes of the Ministry of Health

484 Ministry of Finance - 5.3.1 Tariffs in emerging and developing countries

are needed from tax revenues, the people must vote on it.[485] Private sponsors can be churches and foundations. They can also contribute personnel and material and can make a choice as to where it is used. What funds, personnel and material are used for is determined by law and thus democratically voted on by the people.

8.7.1 Import tariffs[486]

Additional import tariffs apply to goods that a developing country exports even though they are in short supply in the developing country or have higher relative prices than in the donor country. Relative prices mean that, for example, a price in the donor country for bread is low compared to the median per capita income in the donor country. The price of bread may be cheaper in the developing country, but the income of the inhabitants of the developing country is also much lower. Import tariffs raise prices, so fewer goods are exported by the developing country. The amount of import tariffs is a percentage of the value of the goods that corresponds to the production costs in the developing country. The percentage is calculated from the prices of materials and wages in the donor country's domestic market that would be needed to produce the goods. Ultimately, the import tariff makes goods from developing countries as expensive as they are in the donor country.

8.7.2 Export tariffs[487]

Export duties apply to the export of goods that are offered in the developing country at a lower price than the production costs there plus 10% profits. For example, a litre of milk can be produced more cheaply in an industrialised country through industrialised agriculture than in a developing country. If milk powder or milk is exported and sold at a price below the cost-covering price in the developing country, this drives domestic

---

485 Ministry of Finance - 9.5 Budget vote
486 §152,3,4 Tariffs
487 §152,3,4 Tariffs

dairy farmers out of business. Export tariffs raise prices 30% above local production costs.

8.8 Development journeys

The development aid is planned and implemented in development tours through the country together with the local population. The development workers travel through the country with mobile homes and equipment vans, mobile laboratories and construction machinery. Different equipment is carried on different trips, but the mobile homes are used for each trip. Depending on the size of the country, 5 to 10 teams of development workers of 4 persons per motorhome travel along the route set by the embassy.

Development aid is coordinated by the embassy in the country that has been classified as a developing country by the Ministry of Foreign Affairs. Embassy staff put together the team of development workers to suit the level of development of the country. Depending on the level of development and geological conditions in the country, different experts from companies and scientists from the state service are selected. Embassy staff with local knowledge and interpreters accompany the development workers on their development trips through the country.

The embassies from developing countries compile data that tourists from the donor country can collect on their trips and enter it on the embassy's website. Volunteers from the donor country can actively accompany development trips.

8.9 Needs assessment

Whether a country is in need of development aid is researched by the Institute for Development Aid. The state of democratic structures and processes in the country are examined, as well as compliance with human rights, the rule of law, equality, opportunities for social security, integration, education, health and family policy.

Needs assessment tasks are to find strengths and weaknesses

in the country in handling agriculture, infrastructure, energy, water and wastewater management, waste disposal and recycling, school education, health care, party system and self-government.

On the first development journey, the necessary data for the needs assessment are compiled and evaluated. On the waypoints of the given route are existing or to-be-built sewage treatment plants, power plants, waste dumps, schools, hospitals, rivers, lakes, pipelines, roads, railways, town halls and fields. Photos and videos are taken, air, soil and water samples are taken and interviews are conducted. The interviews consist of questions such as: Where is the nearest hospital here? Where is the nearest school? Where is the nearest market? Do you have work? Are you satisfied with it? What training and skills do you have? Children are asked if they go to school, how they find it there, how long they attend school every day and approximately how old they will be when they leave school. The questionnaires are designed by the Institute for Evaluation to suit each region and age group.[488]

The interviews are intended to find eligible persons in order to offer them training or studies in the donor country. To find more applicants, advertising is done on relevant websites, TV programmes, newspapers and billboards.

Every citizen looking for work whom the development workers consider suitable and creditworthy is recorded by name, along with his or her address and contact details. These citizens later serve as economic development workers.

The exploration team of the first development trip consists of scientists and teachers who explore the country. For example, 4 persons with university degrees in either agricultural sciences, environmental sciences, comprehensive school teaching in politics and economics, sports and physics or medicine can be selected. Scientists should bring the expertise to collect data, the analysis of which will be used for the upcoming development journeys. Teachers should bring the experience to identify who is a good student and should receive a scholarship for the education programme.

---

488 Ministry of Labour - 20.10 Institute for Evaluation

8.10 Assistance

The scope of development aid depends on the standard of living, human needs and geological conditions in the developing country, as well as on the consent of the foreign and domestic citizens.

8.10.1 Training programme

In the training programme, persons from the countries with development aid are brought to the donor country to be trained as trainers. They then return home to train professionals in their developing country. The trainings range from Company Auditing Agency auditors to teachers of reading, writing, arithmetic or computer operation. Specific training or study programmes are offered for selected locations. Depending on the expertise needed to develop a place, appropriate volunteers are sought. The needs assessment determines how many farmers, water managers, doctors, teachers, construction workers, rubbish collectors, sewage treatment plant operators or other necessary professions are needed in a place. All these jobs are advertised in the locality. Persons from the locality can apply for them. Applicants with previous experience will be given preference.

Volunteers send their applications to the embassy in their developing country. Applications can be submitted by post or on the embassy's website. On the website, there is a completion guide for the application in the national language. Applications should include letters of motivation in which applicants state why they are seeking the study or training. In the CV, applicants should state their age, interests, education and work experience. Applications must not be longer than 2 A4 pages and are checked at the embassy, translated and sent to the head office in the donor country. There, an algorithm evaluates the data and links suitable persons with suitable educational programmes in suitable educational institutions in the donor country.

Applicants whose applications are accepted are invited to the embassy for interviews. If too few applicants can afford to travel to the interview, embassy staff travel to the cities and interview all applicants from within a 20km radius of the city. Accepted applicants are given a solar-powered laptop through which they first complete a distance learning course.[489] Those who achieve at least a grade 3 in all examinations are allowed to continue their educational programme. Examinations may be repeated up to twice. Those who have passed the theoretical part are allowed to travel to the donor country for 12 months to do practical work for 10 months, take their final exams in the eleventh month and spend another month on holiday in the donor country. If possible, persons from the same hometown spend their stay in the donor country together. The purpose of this is for persons with different qualifications to get to know each other so that they can already get used to working together and support and coordinate with each other in their home country. Afterwards, the graduates return to their country and become trainers and employers for their fellow citizens in their home town.

8.10.2 Infrastructure

The development journey of the construction teams[490] follows the route of the other development workers. Unlike the other teams, however, the construction teams visit each location only once and stay until all construction projects have been completed.
With the help of the infrastructure machines[491] , the construction of roads, bridges, railways, sewage systems, cabling and buildings for education and health is accelerated. Once the state infrastructure and the education and training system in the country are functioning, the construction crews withdraw from the country and the donor country-trained instructors teach the population how to use the new buildings effectively.

---

489 Ministry of Education - 12.6 Global Education
490 Ministry of Infrastructure - 5.8 Construction Team
491 Ministry of Infrastructure - 5.10 Infrastructurators

8.10.3 Politician training

Developing country politicians and domestic people who would like to become politicians receive a scholarship to study political science in the donor country or continent and become involved in a political party. In this way, they learn about the political structures and processes of the dynamic media democracy.[492] During the semester break, they do internships in a state enterprise they choose themselves. On their return, they support the establishment of employers' and employees' representative bodies, clubs and 18 political parties, one for each remit.

8.10.4 Economic development

Economic aid aims to promote employment by making training, business creation and trade sustainable. Sustainability results from training trainers, running companies democratically and cooperatively, and promoting trade in products. Promotion is limited to products made from renewable and naturally occurring resources in developing countries. Through the digital infrastructure established by the Construction Team, digitalisation can be promoted to reach the standard of industrialised countries as quickly as possible.

In order to develop a country economically, basic supply must be ensured. Economic promotion through development aid aims to ensure that the locals take their basic supply into their own hands and run agricultural and craftsperson companies for this purpose.

Before the development workers leave the country, they return for a final farewell visit and document what progress has been made. Through these assessments, the Development Agency can evaluate missions as successfully completed or failed.

The development workers ensure that companies are set up to produce all the goods frequently ordered from the ordering department in the developing country. All supported companies have to give a part of their profits to the cooperatives,

---

492 Ministry of State Organisation - 8 Political structure, 9 Political processes

which together equip factories with machines to produce all necessary goods, so that all cooperatives and their businesses are supported. The machines may be ordered at any time by paying in advance through the ordering department. Delivery is made to the nearest port or airport and must be transported from there to the recipient by a domestic logistics company. A textbook describes and shows in the national language how to make tools for agriculture or crafts, using existing resources in the country. The textbook is available via the Knowledge Directory[493] and can be ordered as a bound edition. The development workers give the voluntary farmers and craftspersons an introduction to the textbook. Those who have received an introduction receive a certificate with which they can apply as journeymen or qualified assistants to returning domestic skilled workers trained in the donor country.

8.10.4.1 Cooperatives

In the course of the needs assessment, persons are sought who would like to found a cooperative together. One of them can participate in the training programme and does internships in cooperatives in the donor country. After their return, the cooperatives are founded. There, they jointly administer their capital in the form of entrance fees, membership fees, machinery and buildings in a direct democratic way. All members have voting rights. Whether members receive more or less voting rights or profit sharing if they have contributed more or less to the cooperative in cash or in kind is decided by all members with equal voting rights.

8.10.4.2 Agriculture

Agriculture development is designed to provide sustainable food security, agriculture and fisheries for the population. Sustainability results from optimal rural development that is adapted to natural resources. In order to be able to optimally cultivate the land, land rights may be redistributed. The

---

493 Ministry of Education - 12.7 Knowledge Directory

deciding factor is that land belongs to individual nationals or to the people, not to foreigners. Forestry is given sufficient forest areas, which are managed with permaculture and also provide sufficient wood, fresh air and moisture. Animal husbandry is carried out in harmony with permaculture on agricultural land and fish farming largely replaces fishing.

8.10.4.2.1 Cultivation planning

All persons who reported to the development workers as willing farmers on the first trip are visited again. Some of them are already participating in the training programme, others are starting to plan and build up agriculture with permaculture in their homeland.[494] In the meantime, the locally taken samples from the first trip have been analysed in the mobile laboratory or in the donor country. On the second trip of the economic development workers, the farmers receive the results of the samples as well as information on which form of agriculture or livestock breeding is possible. They are to agree with the development workers on plants and animals for which seeds or breeding animals are to be cultivated and which agricultural machinery is necessary.

8.10.4.2.2 Agricultural cooperatives

At the end of the cultivation planning discussion, the farmers from a radius of about 20 kilometres are invited to gather on a fixed date to form a cooperative. On this date, all purchases such as seeds, breeding animals and agricultural machinery are ordered. The development workers make sure that plants and animals are adapted to the region and that all farmers as a whole can produce a varied food supply without damaging the soil and water. Competition between farmers that could lead to shortages or rising prices is avoided and economies of scale are exploited. Farms, suppliers and processing industries are organised into a cooperative by all domestic participants to reduce costs and apply democratic administration of capital

---

494 Ministry of Labour - 19.8.7 Nature-based agriculture: permaculture

and labour.

8.10.4.2.3 Procurement of operating resources

The development workers order all goods through the ordering department. The expensive agricultural machinery has to be shared by a cooperative in which each farmer gives a part of his maximum 500 Dollars to the cooperative and thereby receives a right of use. The cooperative undertakes to construct necessary agricultural buildings, such as silos or stables for all its farmers by all its farmers in a fixed period of time until the third visit. As soon as the construction teams have finished building the infrastructure, they help the cooperative to construct new buildings and use farmers as labourers. If there are no building materials or no construction machines available for the construction work, the construction teams can order materials and use their machines. Building materials can be bought on credit and must be paid off after 10 years.
On the third visit, the development workers bring all the ordered goods. They show the farmers how to use the seeds or breeding animals in the new buildings and with the new machines. Based on the evaluated soil samples from their area, farmers receive cultivation plans in their national language on how to cultivate their fields. Domestic farmers who have participated in the training programme return as agronomists and take care of the improvement of all farms in a cooperative and train farmers.

8.10.4.3 Craftsperson

Existing and newly established craft enterprises for the construction and equipping of residential buildings and companies are promoted. Domestic workers willing to work can report to development workers to be included in an Internet-based Labour Directory[495] for the developing country. Workers can join together in groups to set up a business. Existing craft enterprises can hire new workers with suitable

---

495 Ministry of Labour - 13 Labour Directory

skills or motivations. Support is provided in the form of a micro-credit from the ordering department of a maximum of 100 Dollars per employee and entrepreneur. Employees must be employed for as long as the development workers are in the country, but at least for 2 years. This should make it possible for the staff of a company to join forces on an equal footing in order to jointly purchase the jointly desired means of production or devices through democratic voting.

8.10.4.4 Ordering department

All goods consumed by the development aid workers and the locals on behalf of the development aid workers during the development aid are purchased and shipped through the central ordering department of the Ministry of Foreign Affairs. The Procurement Department is a division of the Procurement Office.[496]

The new goods come from the Planned Economy or companies of the Social Market Economy. Used goods from all economic forms of the donor country that are not used in the Planned Economy as well as used goods from the developing country can be included in the order range. If possible, goods are purchased in the developing country. As soon as companies or raw material warehouses that can provide the required goods are found during the needs assessment, the development workers report the addresses, quantities and prices to the ordering department. If raw material deposits have to be developed in order to extract the raw materials, the Construction Team builds the necessary infrastructure.

When issuing goods, care is taken to ensure that the goods are available as quickly as possible and that used goods must first be issued before new goods can be issued. Care must also be taken to ensure that the cooperatives receive new and used goods on an equal basis in order to avoid envy later on.

Each nationals who is allowed to order goods from the ordering department is selected for this purpose by development workers and his or her personal data is reported to the ordering department. The development workers assess

496 Ministry of Labour - 6 Procurement Office

the creditworthiness and the expected turnover of the farmers and craftspersons and can set a credit limit of a maximum of 500 Dollars accordingly. This money can only be invested in goods from the ordering department to start an agriculture or craftsperson business. While the development workers are in the country, ordered goods are delivered from the donor country.

Deliveries are made by a logistics company run by unemployed domestic workers and second-hand vehicles from the donor country. The vehicles can be bought by the domestic employees in a Lease-purchase process after the development workers have left to take over the logistics company in a cooperative.

If all loans have not been repaid by the time the aid workers leave, trade embargoes are imposed after 10 years at the latest, or the local authorities seize the outstanding amounts from the defaulting debtors or deliver them to work in prisons in the donor country, where they work off the defaulting amounts and travel expenses at the applicable minimum wage and are then deported.

After the withdrawal of the aid workers, no more goods may be ordered from the ordering department by nationals. This is because the prices in the catalogue are usually lower than the production costs in the country for equivalent goods. This is the case because the donor country can produce more efficiently in technical terms and therefore more productively, and has second-hand goods that can produce less efficiently than new goods, but are far from broken. As initial equipment, the goods from the order catalogue are supposed to enable the simultaneous start-up of many companies which, in interaction, can quickly repay the loans from the order catalogue on their domestic market. As part of the development aid, a similar procurement operation is set up in the developing country itself so that further enterprises can be set up in the same style on their own.

8.11 End of an aid mission

Aid missions end as soon as the people cut funding for the cost centre of certain projects in the budget or refuse to provide aid to a particular country. Missions also end when the Development Agency considers the aid mission to have ended successfully or to have failed.

Missions can end in failure if the government of the developing country rejects the aid. In this case, when a new government takes office, the embassy also asks it whether development aid will be allowed or supported.

Rejection by the local population occurs when the people of a developing country reach the 50% quorum. Then at least 50% of the population have signed up on lists to reject projects or the entire operation in their country. The lists for the quorum must be publicly available in the town halls of the countries and regions where development aid is provided. The lists are stored in a voting computer of the Ministry of Foreign Affairs in laptop form. Those who sign up for a list must give their fingerprint on the reader on the computer and have their face photographed by the voting computer's camera. The voting computer automatically checks whether this person has already voted on this or another voting computer and refuses entries in the list if necessary. These lists include all development aid, i.e. all ongoing projects in the country. Each project can be rejected individually. However, the entire list can also be deselected across the board. If the quorum of 50% is reached for a project, only that project is discontinued.

8.12 Continental development policy

In the short term, development aid focuses on developing structurally weak areas domestically so that the new procedures, staff and devices are tested domestically. Once the structurally weak areas have been successfully developed inland, development aid workers move through willing International Union member states and then through International Union candidate countries where the population has agreed to development aid. Other International Union member states may participate in the development assistance model.

In addition to buildings for education and infrastructure, economic development is also promoted. In areas with high unemployment, start-ups in a cooperative, similar to Mondragon[497] , can be promoted through the construction of office buildings and factories as well as training in enterprise policy. If the population of the country agrees, a hybrid economic system[498] can also be installed so that unemployed people can earn a living in the Planned Economy.

The development workers determine the level of development and propose various development options to the affected population. Development aid on one's own continent ends when all the states of the future unified states of the continent are sufficiently developed to be able to achieve the same standard of living.

Development aid on its own continent will develop all underdeveloped regions within the next 5 to 25 years and promote the construction of the transcontinental route.[499] In order to be able to send supplies for development aid across the continent, the route that will be completed by then will be used. This route connects the northern, southern, eastern and western ends of the continent.

8.13 International development policy

International development policy is democratised and restructured in the course of communitarisation. It changes its approach so that neighbouring states and member states of the same International Union support each other with development aid until equality of opportunity is established. International development aid, in which the entire community of states is involved at the same time, is limited to humanitarian aid in emergencies caused by natural disasters and wars.

At the international level, the United Nations is responsible for global development aid. In the course of communitarisation,

497 https://www.mondragon-corporation.com/
498 Ministry of Labour - 8 Theory of Hybrid Economic Systems
499 Ministry of Infrastructure - 6.2 Underground networks, 8.8.4 Tunnel railway, 8.8.3 Maglev railway

the responsibilities and activities for development cooperation at the OECD are transferred to the United Nations.

All nations that provide development aid coordinate their measures in the United Nations Conference on Trade and Development (UNCTAD)[500] . Developing countries are also involved in the conference. The aim of coordination is to ensure that all developing countries are similarly developed, that no country pays or receives more per capita, and that all developing countries can foresee when it is their turn and which industrialised nation will provide them with aid.

The Development Assistance Committee (DAC)[501] is responsible for the control of standards and services as well as the provision of financial, technical and human resources for state development cooperation. It coordinates the work of the Development Agencies in the participants' countries.

International development policy is executed by the Ministry of Foreign Affairs in cooperation with the United Nations. The Development Agency of the Ministry of Foreign Affairs is responsible for this. In the course of continental communitarisation, participation in international development aid becomes part of the area of accountability of Continental Union foreign policy.

In the course of international communitarisation, the DAC merges into the Development Agency and the Institute for Development Aid. The International Court of Justice becomes responsible for violations and the settlement of disputes in development aid.

8.13.1 World Bank

The World Bank[502] is responsible for providing money for development financing. In the course of the communitarisation of the continents, it can be joined by other multi-state development banks, such as the Asian Infrastructure Investment Bank (AIIB)[503] . It also takes over the tasks of

---

500https://unctad.org/
501https://www.oecd.org/dac/
502https://www.worldbank.org/en/home
503https://www.aiib.org/en/index.html

the Paris Club[504] , the International Monetary Fund (IMF)[505] and the International Fund for Agricultural Development (IFAD)[506] . The World Bank takes over the debt reduction and pays off the donor countries. It converts any assets from development funds into a development fund, the proceeds of which are used to finance international development aid. This means that indebted developing countries pay for development aid with their interest. Customs duties on trade with developing countries provide the interim financing.

8.13.2 Humanitarian aid

In addition to planned development aid, which moves all around the neighbouring countries, there is also spontaneous humanitarian aid. Humanitarian aid always comes into play when sudden humanitarian crises occur. Such crises can be triggered by natural disasters or wars. Humanitarian aid serves post-conflict rehabilitation through stabilisation with measures of development aid. This is intended to combat the causes of flight and manage crises. Infrastructure in a crisis context consists of transitional aid for reconstruction. This includes military evacuation of the population, resettlement in refugee camps and self-reliant operation of the camps by Planned Economy. The UN Peacekeeping forces secure the convoy that brings the civilian population out of the danger zone into refugee camps. The United Nations negotiates locations for the refugee camps with neighbouring states and parties to the conflict. The refugee camps must have arable land and a water supply so that the camp can support itself. All services that are administered by the state in the social and Asylum Villages with Planned Economy must be organised by the residents of the camp themselves, but they also receive plans for implementation in their national language and programmes for digital administration.[507]

---

504 https://clubdeparis.org/
505 https://www.imf.org/en/Home
506 https://www.ifad.org/en/
507 Ministry of Planned Economy - Complete, except Mobile Social Village and disaster management, Ministry of Integration - 8.6.1 Asylum Village

The United Nations High Commissioner for Refugees (UNHCR)[508] offers tent cities, which are delivered by convoys of the United Nations Peacekeeping[509] . They also evacuate the population and bring them to the camps. In the camp, the refugees, under the guidance of experienced marshals, first set up the tents and sanitary facilities. Then, one after the other, the inhabitants build their homes and supply centres together, using raw materials from the surrounding area and support from military pioneer units of United Nations Peacekeeping. The tent city is then dismantled and the United Nations Peacekeeping troops leave. Afterwards, agricultural areas around the camp are cultivated with permaculture. As soon as it is possible for the refugees to return, the United Nations Peacekeeping will newly come and bring the refugees back. The camps with all their buildings and fields are left as a gift to the population of the host country.

In the course of communitarisation, humanitarian aid is no longer administered intergovernmentally, but centrally by the United Nations. The Development Agency organises the humanitarian aid contribution in cooperation with the ministries of security and integration.

8.13.2.1 Natural disasters

In the event of severe natural disasters in other countries, the disaster management[510] sends its reserve troops to the affected areas. These cases are used as exercises for the civil protection reservists. Participation is voluntary and is compensated as paid special leave if the citizens provide tax money for it in the budget vote.

8.13.2.2 War zones

Refugees from war zones can apply for asylum at the embassy in their country of origin or a neighbouring country and go through the asylum procedure. They return from the Asylum

---

508 https://www.unhcr.org/
509 https://peacekeeping.un.org/en
510 Ministry of Security - 5.7 Disaster management

Villages[511] with the skills to build houses, pipelines and transport routes, to be able to support themselves with the most basic necessities and to organise their coexistence in a direct democratic way. Asylum seekers who have been granted asylum may apply for development aid from the embassy in their country of origin. This development aid consists of funds that were also used in the Asylum Village to produce prefabricated houses, modules for traffic routes and pipelines. The necessary factory equipment can either be rented or bought. The rent must be paid on return and depends on the useful life, wear and tear and the new price of the equipment. The purchase is a hire-purchase scheme with an interest rate equal to the inflation rate of the Social Market Economy's national currency. The term ends after 10 years at the latest.

8.14 Continental development aid

All unified states, which will exist in the medium term in 50 to 100 years, engage in joint coordinated development aid for underdeveloped states or continents. They vote on who is responsible for which territory and take on sponsorships for other continents or countries that border or lie on their continent and still need development aid. Since the unified states are larger than individual countries, several developing countries can be developed simultaneously by their respective sponsors.

The unified continental states compensate their neighbouring continent in the medium term for past exploitation. All citizens of the exploited continent can participate in the education programme in order to travel to the exploiting continent after passing their correspondence course. There they are then allowed to finish the studies they have started and return home.

---

511 Ministry of Integration - 8.6.1 Asylum Village

8.14.1 Business start-up programme

The continental business start-up programme for the neighbouring underdeveloped continent corresponds to the conventional training programme, but additionally for business founders. The difference is also that all inhabitants of the neighbouring continent can apply at the same time. The embassies of all donor countries in the developing countries receive the applications and send them translated to their respective Ministry of Foreign Affairs. There, all the data is entered. From the data obtained, an algorithm is to search the needs and business plans of all applicants in their place of residence and simulate and predict a resulting development. It checks which training courses are most likely to be needed for the local circumstances. This data comes from development trips where development workers have done a needs assessment. The applicant and development worker data sets are combined to have an economic simulation for the next 5, 10 and 100 years calculated by the algorithm[512] . The simulation is repeated until the total number of applicants and their educational programmes match the conditions in the country. Conditions are the local conditions, the demand of the local population and all the educational qualifications necessary to run companies that cover the basic supply of the citizens. As a result, applicants may be asked whether they would also complete a different but similar educational programme and run a different but similar company. This is the only way to ensure that there is no surplus of certain skilled workers but a shortage of skilled workers in other sectors. Digital calculation links raw material deposits with extracting, processing, supplying and purchasing companies that provide vital goods or services.

The aim of development aid through the business start-up programme is for the developing country to be able to support itself with all basic supply goods and services after development aid. Basic supply consists of the provision of food, housing, textiles, health, energy, state organisation and democracy. Examples of basic supply provision can be

---

512 Ministry of Digital Affairs - 15.3 Algoracle

observed in all Social Villages[513] and viewed through reports on Social Villages from the Party Television and looked up in the Knowledge Directory.[514]

8.14.1.1 Waiting list

Suitable applicants receive places on waiting lists because it is impossible to admit all applicants from the developing country to educational institutions on the donor continent at the same time and it makes sense to provide economic and infrastructural development aid in the applicant's place of residence in a timely manner. They can shorten their waiting time by pursuing an educational programme for which there is an unfilled vacancy. This may require a move or a change of application to another educational programme. On the donor continent page, all educational institutions indicate how many vacancies they have in educational programmes that are necessary for the development of the developing country. The waiting period may be longer if the donor continent has a high demand for skilled workers or if many nationals of the donor continent wish to follow the educational programmes in question.

8.14.1.2 Order

The locations that will be developed first are along the transcontinental route. The training programme gives preference to applicants from regions along the transcontinental route so that the construction teams can already draw on a population of home-grown skilled workers. This enables additional craftspersons from the developing country who have been trained in the donor continent to provide support assistance in the construction of the transcontinental route. Afterwards, supply chains can be established via the supply routes and gradually the remaining regions can be included in the business start-up programme.

---

513 Ministry of Planned Economy - 9 Work area basic supply
514 Ministry of Education - 12.7 Knowledge Directory

8.14.1.3 Stay in the country of training

Once accepted, applicants will receive a training visa and a travel voucher for their journey. The return travel tickets are developed and purchased in the training country by the trainees, at the latest by the expiry date of the visa. The accepted applicants travel to the member states of the International Union or the United States of the Continents to the participating companies or educational institutions. There they receive the local wage to organise their own living expenses or a stipend. In the training country, they live in the asylum house[515] of a Social Village and are also trained in the Social Village. At the end of their regular training, they still have to complete a trainer course. After that, they fly back to their homeland and look for capable and willing people there to train them. If production machines are needed for their work, which cannot be produced immediately in the country of origin, they are produced in the country of training and sold to the trainers. They have to pay back the purchase amount in instalments as soon as they earn money with it.

8.14.1.4 Further aids

Graduates of the business start-up programme or the training programme can request new assistance if progress is demonstrably made while the development workers are still in the country or have not yet been to the region. This is done, for example, by graduates reporting a need for specific teachers trained through the training programme in the donor continent to independently build a school for the teachers during the training period or to be assisted in the construction by the development workers' Construction Team.

---

515 Ministry of Planned Economy - 12.3.10 House of asylum seekers, 18.5 Asylum

8.15 Long-term perspective

Development aid on Earth ends in the long term in about 200 years, when all Earth's citizens live on one standard of living. As soon as a new Earth-like planet is discovered, it will be developed through development aid from the Ministry of Foreign Affairs.

9 Asylum application procedure[516]

Asylum is granted within the capacities set by the people in the budget vote[517] and the quota of foreigners. The Ministry of Foreign Affairs is responsible for the asylum application procedure. For deportation, the embassies conduct the negotiations for orderly repatriation. The Ministry of Integration is responsible for residence in the domestic country and for determining the quota of foreigners in the domestic country.[518]

Embassies assess the danger situation in the foreign country in order to check whether nationals of that country can be granted asylum because they are politically persecuted or threatened with death. They coordinate the entry for asylum applicants through an asylum application. They work together with the Integration Agency for this purpose.[519]

If a country becomes unsafe for the entire population or for entire regions in the short term due to war or natural disasters, asylum seekers find refuge near their home country. The United Nations humanitarian aid is responsible for this type of accommodation. Asylum is granted for longer-term accommodation.

---

516 §162,6 Foreign affairs: BV Art. 54, §243,1 Legislation on foreigners and asylum: BV Art. 121
517 Ministry of Finance - 9.5 Budget vote
518 Ministry of Integration - 8.4 Asylum procedures, 7.4 Quota of foreigners
519 Ministry of Integration - 5 Integration Agency

9.1 Uncertain countries of origin

Each domestic embassy prepares an annual assessor's report for the foreign country of origin in which it is based as to whether the country is classified as an unsafe country of origin. It bases this on the reports of asylum applicants and its own observations. Residents can be politically persecuted, there is a war or civil war. Disasters can also make a country an unsafe country of origin. The Minister of Foreign Affairs ultimately decides whether a country is classified as unsafe.

As soon as asylum applicants enter from this country, the total number of asylum seekers who are nationals of this country is reported to the country every year. There is an obligation to take them back, otherwise sanctions follow, such as trade embargoes, special tariffs or travel restrictions. As soon as a country of origin is considered unsafe, no military equipment may be delivered to that country. The ambassador reports annually to the Ministry of Foreign Affairs of the unsafe country of origin on the reasons why its nationals have been granted asylum. The questionnaire of the asylum application also includes what suggestions for improvement the asylum seekers would have for their country of origin so that they would return. An anonymised copy of this also goes to the United Nations ambassador, who can use this evidence to promote sanctions or relief efforts in that country.

The embassy checks when unsafe countries of origin are safe again, which ends the asylum procedure. In voting with the Ministry of Foreign Affairs of the country of origin, the return of the asylum seekers is organised. The Ministry of Foreign Affairs of the country of origin receives information about what the asylum seekers have learned in the Asylum Village.

9.2 Asylum application in embassies

Asylum applicants must go to the embassy where their language is spoken or the foreign language that asylum applicants can speak. Interpreters are the exception. Asylum must be applied for in an embassy of a country that is not a member of the Continental Union or later of the united states of the continent. Asylum applicants who want to leave the country do not have to visit the embassy in the country where they are politically persecuted or permanently threatened with death. This is also possible in embassies in neighbouring countries. There are many other countries that also grant asylum. So when an asylum applicant chooses this country as his destination, he knows that as an asylum seeker in the Asylum Village he will have to work for the reconstruction of his home country, together with his compatriots of his Asylum Village.[520] If an asylum applicant decides to become a naturalised citizen after initial reception, he knows that he must adapt to the domestic culture in order to become a naturalised citizen.[521] Whether and to what extent refugees are allowed to care for their old culture depends on the host family and the place of residence.

9.2.1 Waiting time

Each embassy that accepts asylum applicants displays how long the waiting time is for the individual steps until departure. The display shows the next available appointment at the PC terminal, how long the processing time currently is between the asylum application being submitted and the video interview, and how long it took for the last asylum seeker at this embassy from the first appointment to departure. The display is on the home page of the embassy's website and on a display board attached to the outside of the embassy.

9.2.2 First appointment

An appointment for the asylum application can be made online. To do this, one selects the website of the embassy where the asylum application is to be taken up and all subsequent appointments take place. Appointments for the responsible embassy can also be made by telephone or in person at an embassy or consulate. At the first appointment, only the asylum application is filled out and a second appointment is made by

---

520 Ministry of Integration - 8.6 Asylum seekers
521 Ministry of Integration - 8.5 Refugees

which date the asylum application has been examined.

9.2.2.1 Data collection

The asylum application can only be filled in at the embassy's PC terminal. It is necessary to fill it out at the embassy in order to see whether the asylum applicant has written his statements himself and is not lying. For this purpose, one PC terminal is located in each of the opaque telephone booths. The PC terminal is equipped with a wide-angle camera, a microphone, fingerprint scanner and a lie detector. The camera records the input process to ensure that the asylum applicant fills out the application alone and without any aids and whether he or she shows gestures or external signs that suggest lying. The microphone records any sounds the asylum applicant makes, detects signs of determination or uncertainty, converts the spoken word into text and translates it. The fingerprint scanner is used for identification and matching with the police query via the Security Directory. The lie detector is connected to the asylum applicant and measures brain waves, heart rate, breathing rate and sweat production. Hair samples are taken as proof of origin and age and an X-ray of the dentition is taken.

A programme automatically recognises these signs, evaluates them and transmits them to the responsible embassy staff and asylum examiner in the examination report.

On each PC, the first thing that can be selected is the language. Only one programme is installed. The programme starts with the video recording function. A digital vote asks questions and the respondents are filmed for a maximum of 60 minutes. This is followed by the open and closed questionnaire function. It is also about what motivated the humans to flee and what suggestions for improvement would have to be implemented so that they do not leave the country. Typed texts are translated automatically. Spoken language is immediately displayed in text form in the set native language as it is spoken. Faults in the speech recognition programme must be corrected immediately via the keyboard. This means that some information must be typed in, clicked on or spoken freely into the camera. The answers are evaluated by software and appropriate questions are asked. This questionnaire is created by the asylum examiners at the Ministry of Foreign Affairs in the capital city. The software comes from the Ministry of Digital Affairs[522] . Through this questionnaire, asylum applications are rejected, accepted or sent to the individual case examination. After saving, suggested appointments are displayed, from which the asylum applicant must choose one. Finally, each asylum applicant is asked whether and how he or she would like to be contacted by the embassy if his or her motions have been rejected, so that he or she can avoid going to the embassy. If the contact details are not to be used for contacting, the rejected asylum applicant will only receive the news on the agreed second date.

9.2.2.2 Reasons for refusal

If the evaluation of the information revealed that there is no entitlement to asylum, the application will be rejected. This may be the case, for example, if the police check reveals that the asylum applicant is wanted in the Country-of-destination or in a country that is in an International Union or has already been convicted of a criminal law offence there. For this purpose, the personal data provided, fingerprints, DNA from the hair sample and the image of the face are checked against all entries in the Security Directory .[523]
If the reasons for the flight do not meet the criteria of an unsafe country of origin, the motions are also rejected. The criteria for an unsafe country of origin are set by the Minister of Foreign Affairs in a People's Committee[524] and each embassy checks whether the countries in which they are based meet the criteria in full, in part or not at all.
Anyone who lies when making an application is also not entitled to asylum.
All this data is digitally recorded and automatically evaluated.

---

522 Ministry of Digital Affairs - 13.3.1 Software creation
523 Ministry of Security - 4.6 Security Directory
524 Ministry of State Organisation - 9.6 Committee

If undoubted reasons for rejection are found, a motions is automatically rejected. Appeals are not possible and legal process is excluded.

9.2.3 Second appointment

If the asylum application has not been automatically rejected and the questionnaire has resulted in an asylum claim, the recorded video of the questionnaire is automatically translated, proofread by an embassy staff member and sent to the capital city. There, the asylum auditors of the Ministry of Foreign Affairs check it.

At the second appointment, the embassy staff member or interpreter who had previously read the application for proofreading and the asylum applicant(s) at the embassy conduct an internet-based video call with an asylum examiner inland.

9.2.3.1 Video interview

The embassy staff member or interpreter translates the asylum applicant's statements for the asylum examiner. Interpreters may only be used if the asylum applicant was not able to file his asylum application at the embassy where the embassy staff speak his language. At the beginning, all documents such as passports, identity cards and certificates are checked for authenticity, photographed and digitised and inserted into the asylum application.

The asylum applicant may be of any age and bring his or her first-degree family with him or her if the motions contain the necessary information. All persons who are said to be at risk are interviewed individually. If all statements match and in-depth questions were answered similarly or identically, the statements are considered to be true. If all the information provided contains grounds for claiming asylum and the country of origin is deemed too unsafe for these humans, the asylum application will be granted.

The asylum examiners are located in the capital city of the

Ministry of Foreign Affairs in a telephone centre. They first check the asylum application, which was sent as an email from the embassy, followed by the interview. At the end of the interview, the asylum applicants have to leave the room briefly so that the asylum examiners and the embassy staff can have a final consultation to reach their verdict. The asylum applicant is then immediately informed of the decision. If the asylum application has been rejected, no new application for asylum may be made unless the reasons for danger change or the country of origin is declared by the Minister of Foreign Affairs to be an unsafe country of origin for all inhabitants.

9.2.3.2 Departure preparation

If the asylum application is approved, the asylum applicant is given the status of "asylum seeker". At the embassy's travel agency, an asylum card is produced for every asylum seeker of any age with the personal data already given in the asylum application. In addition, a recent photograph is taken, fingerprints are taken and the iris is scanned. In the travel agency there is a check-card printing machine that loads all the data onto the chip in the card and prints the front page with a photograph and name, date of birth, place of birth and the heading "Asylum seeker". After the identity card has been handed to the asylum seeker, he or she must immediately sign it under the eyes of an embassy employee. The signature is checked against the one on the asylum application. For children up to the age of ten, the signature is replaced by a fingerprint. The personal data is sent in encrypted form via the Internet and transmitted to Customs[525] . The asylum card is valid as an entry visa.

Now every asylum seeker has the election whether to organise the trip himself or to book it through the embassy's travel agency. For persons, air travel is offered and freight is sent via an internationally active domestic forwarding agency. The embassy makes all the bookings, not the asylum seeker. However, it is a prerequisite that the asylum seeker has enough money for the outward and return flight and, if necessary, for

525 Ministry of Security - 8.2 Border Protection

the freight transport. If there is not enough money, there is a waiting list until a charter plane becomes full. Those who cannot cover their own travel costs must develop them during their asylum stay and pay them to the Ministry of Foreign Affairs. In order to be able to afford the travel costs, workers are allowed to work in the Social Market Economy and Free Market Economy until the amount is reached.

9.3 Long-term perspective

In order to make asylum unnecessary in the long term, in the medium term all unified states stop exporting weapons and goods at dumping prices for import into unsafe countries of origin.

All arms supplies and tax-subsidised exports at dumping prices to unsafe countries of origin are stopped as soon as possible. The Continental Union ensures that resources and labour in unsafe countries of origin are not exploited. An example of such exploitation is the export of milk powder to Africa, which destroys the local dairy industry through dumping prices. Thus, a litre of milk made from tax-subsidised milk powder from Europe is cheaper than a litre of milk produced in Africa without tax subsidies and without technical and chemical aids. Another example is oil production in West Africa, which is carried out by European corporations without European environmental standards. The results are environmental destruction and the expropriation of the people's property in mineral resources.

In the course of communitarisation, asylum becomes unnecessary. States increasingly unify, grant democratic rights to their citizens, conclude peace treaties and reduce their armies. Overpopulation is avoided by lowering the birth rate through prosperity. In addition, the colonisation of Earth-like planets and living space on Earth above and below water provides additional settlement areas. The people have the opportunity to democratically vote on the demographic development of the population at any time.[526]

526Ministry of Integration - 6.2 Demography

10 End of the Ministry of Foreign Affairs[527]

The work of this ministry will cease in the long term once the tasks of communitarisation, development aid and asylum have been fulfilled.

The Ministry of State Organisation oversees all ministries so that the municipal and national levels can communicate and cooperate. The Ministry of Foreign Affairs coordinates continental policy until all Continental Union member states have joined the inner ring of the Continental Union, i.e. the united states of the continent. From then on, there will only be the continental Ministry of Foreign Affairs. The continental Ministry of Foreign Affairs finally ceases its service when all the states of the world have joined the inner ring of the global Union, i.e. the united states of the world. At the international level, there is a ministry for development aid until all countries are equally developed. As soon as the Ministry of Integration has been communitarised internationally and there are no more embassies, it also takes over the asylum application procedure.

If alien intelligent life forms are found, the Ministry of Foreign Affairs resumes its work and begins democratic negotiations with the aliens.

11 Switching to the new system

The Ministry of Foreign Affairs is responsible for democratising cooperation with foreigners or, if that is not possible, for ending it. All international organisations and intergovernmental meetings at which binding agreements are reached have not yet been democratically legitimised. The background is that heads of state and government are not directly elected or do not have sole authority to exercise law-making, law-speaking, law-executing and law-mediating power. There is a lack of directly elected representatives of the separate powers at the international political level as a whole. In order to ensure peace and prosperity, the people can allow exceptions. The foreign minister asks the affected peoples for permission through voting or risk deselection.

---

527 §168.5 World peace

11.1 Conversion of embassy work

Embassies are given new roles in communitarisation, development aid and the asylum process. Embassies reduce their economic support activities, especially for large multinational corporations.

11.2 Introduction of communitarisation

Communitarisation represents a new orientation of continental policy. The Minister of Foreign Affairs asks all responsible ministers of the surrounding states whether they would like to participate in a continental communitarisation using the International Union procedure. If this meets with approval, the changeover takes place with all voluntary states. A referendum on the project must be held in each participating state.

11.3 Conversion of development aid

Ongoing state financial and personnel participation in development aid shall cease immediately. All funds are spent on building up a task force of full-time and part-time development workers and on purchasing or building their operational equipment. The first test mission develops all underdeveloped regions within the country. Humanitarian aid within the framework of the United Nations remains unaffected, and the commitment there remains unchanged.

11.4 Transitions in the asylum sector

The causes of flight for asylum applicants, which are caused by the receiving country itself, will be stopped immediately. These include arms deliveries and food exports at dumping prices. Asylum applications may only be submitted through embassies with immediate effect. The digitalised asylum procedure will be established as soon as possible.

11.5 Compensations

The state compensation for the consequences of the two world wars is stopped immediately. Further claims are not serviced. The state stops all benefits and payments in order to protect the coming generation. The background to this is that there is no one alive today who is responsible for the suffering that was inflicted. Inherited debt is generally considered inadmissible. Legal process remains possible for the conviction of individual perpetrators, provided the offence is not already time-barred.

11.6 War Graves Convention

The war graves agreements are dissolved and transformed into peace treaties. The Ministry of Foreign Affairs uses its power and financial resources to make peace and not to engage in symbolic politics.

11.7 Changeover of the Tracing Service

All archival material on genocides will be transferred to the national library and made available digitally via the internet. Other states that have committed genocide will also be encouraged to set up a tracing service that will be available to those affected or survivors for 75 years, after which its files will be published in a publicly accessible library and on the internet for their own research.

11.8 Secrecy agreement

Inter-state secrecy agreements are lifted, except for the communitarisation of criminal law investigations and police records systems. Data on ongoing investigations by public prosecutors, Customs and police are exchanged between the communitarised states and classified as secret. The secrecy agreement regulates which degrees of secrecy exist and how secret data may be handled in the contracting states.[528] Like

---

528 https://fragdenstaat.de/anfrage/geheimschutzabkommen-mit-australien/22117/anhang/Australien.pdf

all intergovernmental treaties, this treaty must be submitted to the voting of the affected peoples. Secret agreements that are themselves classified as secret become null and void. No more secret data may then be exchanged with that state until a democratic secret protection agreement has been voted on by a majority.

11.9 Foreigners in the domestic armed forces

Foreigners are not allowed to be inland unless they are a headquarters of a defence alliance or forces of the Continental Defence Army[529] . Once the Continental Defence Army is established, its member states will join or establish the global defence alliance if it does not already exist. All state funding of foreigner forces inland will cease.

11.10 End of foreign missions

The army and police are immediately withdrawn from all foreign missions. From now on, the military will be involved exclusively in United Nations peacekeeping missions with its blue helmet soldiers, armed with lethal weapons.

11.10.1 Withdrawal from war zones

Military operations in war and crisis zones will be discontinued. The domestic and foreigner population will be put to a voting choice on how the withdrawal should take place. The first option is the immediate withdrawal of all troops from the country. The second option is the reconstruction of all infrastructure destroyed in the war, such as buildings, transport routes and supply networks, and the securing of construction sites by remaining soldiers. Scholarships are given to affected foreigners to train skilled workers at schools and colleges inland, who want to work in the buildings, such as hospitals, schools, building material factories or handicraft workshops, when they are completed. The training period that

---

529 Ministry of Security - 9.3.1 Continental Defence Army

the domestic workers spend in the training country lasts as long as the construction of the infrastructure. As soon as the construction work is finished, all workers of the construction team[530] and all soldiers of the army or Continental Defence Army leave the country.

Depending on which option receives the majority of votes, it is carried out. The people can veto the second option. As soon as a quorum of 50% is met or the costs are rejected in the budget vote, the second option is dropped.

11.11 Diplomatic gifts

Gifts and handwritten letters for which the calligraphic service is required are waived. Foreigners are also requested to refrain from such attentions when diplomats and politicians visit the country.

11.12 Financial crisis resolution

Affected states devalue their own currency. If the banking sector is affected, affected states set up a "good bank" in which all valuable securities and debt instruments that remain after the bankruptcy of banks are bundled. Iceland's procedure is considered a model.[531]

11.13 Conversion of the old ministries

For the conversion of the old ministries, all departments and units of the old ministries that are changing to this ministry are identified. The organigrams are used to determine whether an entire department and all its units are changing or only individual units. All unsuitable departments and units are dropped. The existing staff adapts its tasks to the new requirements.

---

530 Ministry of Infrastructure - 5.8 Construction Team
531 https://de.wikipedia.org/wiki/Islands_
Finanzkrise_2008%E2%80%932011

Contact form

Dear reader
If you would like to make what you have read come true, in whole or in part, together with other like-minded people, I offer you several possibilities with this contact form. Fill it out, tear out the page and send it by post to:
Andreas Seidl, P.O. Box 1206, 63488 Seligenstadt / Germany

Or send the details to:
Phone: 0049 1522 818 2243 (whatsapp, telegram, signal)
Email: andreas.seidl2022@web.de

Please mark with a cross:
O   I want to found a dynamic People's Party.
O   I want to donate money for implementation.
O   I want contacts with like-minded people in my area.

Forename: _______________________________________

Surname: _______________________________________

Please fill in only the contact option through which a reply should be made.

Street, house no.:   _______________________________________

Postcode, city, country: _______________________________________

Phone: _______________________________________

Email address: _______________________________________